Relentless Focus:

27 Small Tweaks to Beat Procrastination, Skyrocket Productivity, Outsmart Distractions, Do More in Less Time

By Patrick King
Social Interaction Specialist and Conversation Coach
www.PatrickKingConsulting.com

Table of Contents

Introduction

Many people experience cold feet (or abject fear) about quitting their day jobs and striking out on their own. It is, after all, a considerable financial risk which only becomes greater the older you get. The better you are currently doing, the more you have to lose.

I, on the other hand, couldn't wait to take the leap. I couldn't wait to start working on a beach with my laptop in one hand and a piña colada in the other. I'd seen it on Instagram, so it had to be true. The idea of having total freedom to set my own hours and work environment was so alluring that I ignored all the potential downsides.

As a lawyer, I used to be shackled to my desk for a prescribed period of time. It didn't matter whether I was productive, playing Minesweeper, or just twiddling my thumbs; my presence was the ticket, and the subsequent ride was boring and uninspiring. As long as I finished my assignments before their deadlines, I could collect my paycheck twice a month and clock out.

Most of my waking hours were spent in that stupor, and it was beginning to feel like a poor use of my time, to say the least. I really didn't have to concentrate for any extended period of time, and my productivity could best be characterized as "adequate."

I figured that by working for myself, I could make every minute count and work more efficiently by avoiding bureaucracy, bloated departments, and pointless meetings. In theory, I would be able to do much more in far less time, and spend the rest of my time living my glorious life.

Those warm, fuzzy feelings vanished when, two months after I'd taken the leap, I realized I had generated exactly *zero revenue*.

It turns out that to be productive you need structure and discipline—two things I discovered were not easily achievable on my own.

The exact freedom I cherished was the very thing that made productivity so difficult. Working on your own terms means you are also your sole source of motivation. This presents a problem when what you *really* want to do is play beach volleyball.

Without external motivation and no one to answer to, I was tasked with enforcing deadlines, defeating procrastination, and figuring out how to focus on the task at hand all on my own.

When I really needed to email a client back or calculate the numbers for my business expenses, I inevitably found something that needed to be scrubbed shiny and clean.

So out of necessity, I started a period of research and self-experimentation to discover how to improve my focus and productivity. Humans aren't innately motivated, so what means of external motivation could I create to push myself?

Many late nights later, I had created personal systems that essentially guaranteed my productivity on a daily basis. That's what Relentless Focus is about.

I want to bring to you the wide range of productivity methods I experimented with to supercharge my output and efficiency and claw my business back into the black in record time. There was some overlap and some conflict, but I used myself as a human guinea pig to discover exactly what combination of methods worked best and got me off my butt.

Sometimes the smallest tweaks yielded the greatest results, and methods that other people swore by just didn't resonate or had too steep a learning curve. After all, the

<u>most effective method is one you'll actually use</u>.

This book is broken into five sections, and each section represents a different problem we all have regarding focus. Which area are you struggling with? All of them? There is truly something for everyone here.

Using the methods within, my output skyrocketed while I worked fewer hours, which translated into more hours playing beach volleyball. For entrepreneurs or small business owners, these skills are especially crucial because their time is valuable in a quantifiable way. Time is money!

Yet there's not a person in the world that can't benefit from improving their focus and punching out procrastination. You'll be surprised by how great it feels to have that extra gear in your pocket when you are down to the wire.

Section 1.Take the First Step

For many of us, the act of focusing may not be the difficult part. Often, the difficult part is breaking through the inertia you've been accumulating and just getting started.

This is largely the same in any area or field. For instance, take the literal example of a car. For a car to start, a complex series of explosions have to occur in order to propel pistons into motion. Only then can a car budge forward an inch. However, the second and third inches are far easier because momentum has already been built and inertia has been destroyed.

Unfortunately, we are in states of inertia and rest far more often than not. We struggle to take the first step, even if we might excel once we are in motion. In fact, we actively run from it through procrastination and avoidance. This is going to be the natural first step in creating relentless focus—because you can't create it if you can't get off your butt!

For those of us who end up cleaning our bathrooms and vacuuming our carpets when the time comes, this section is focused on those small tweaks that allow you to fearlessly and quickly take first steps toward anything.

#1. Newton's Law of Momentum

Let's set the scene: You have a big task due and you probably should have started a lot earlier. You know what has to be done, but every time you try to start, you hit a roadblock or something gets in the way, and you've found yourself making no progress. More often than not, you end up vacuuming or cleaning your bathroom. If those are already sparkling clean, you suddenly come up with a host of other things that keep you occupied, but really just amount to wasted motion.

Sound familiar? Luckily, our good friend and famed physicist Isaac Newton can help us out.

Newton's First Law of Motion:
"An object at rest stays at rest and an object in motion stays in motion."

What does this have to do with taking the first step and breaking through your inertia? To boost your productivity and stop falling into these slumps of unproductiveness, get in motion and stay in motion. This begins from the moment you wake up, and over the course of your day, you'll find that you can become like a snowball rolling downhill and only pick up speed.

The first few hours of your day often determine how the rest of it will go, so get up on the right side of bed and start being productive as soon as you can. Set the tone for the kind of day you want to have and create motion for yourself as soon as possible, otherwise it's too easy to end up watching videos and reading entertainment news for hours—because that's the inertia-filled tone you've set for the day. Become the object that is constantly in motion, versus the object that has to summon up the massive amount of willpower to change your status quo.

Here are a few things you can do to have the best type of morning for productivity and momentum.

Plan everything. There is no use waking up ready for a productive day and then spending 30 minutes looking for a shirt that has mysteriously gone missing, or even trying to put your day's tasks into order. Whatever inertia you may have shed you are just being weighed down by again. <u>Plan everything the night before so you can exercise as little brainpower in the morning as possible and hit the ground running</u>.

Get your outfit ready, your breakfast ready, and everything you need to take to work or school ready. Write down your focus or work objectives the night before and have a clear idea of exactly what you will be doing down to the smallest detail. The less thinking, the better! The most productive morning is one where you wake up and are instantly able to take action instead of staying still and making decisions—that's where we tend to fall off-track in regard to taking the first step.

Don't snooze your alarm clock. It's tempting, so very tempting, but you *know* five more minutes can so easily turn into 30, and so easily mean that you are late for something important. Even if you have a day off, plan to wake up at a reasonable hour. It might seem like a small thing, but think of the morning hours wasted without an alarm. You are consciously making a choice, and we see again that allowing yourself space is allowing yourself room for self-sabotage.

You're also committing to starting your day with an act of self-discipline and focus. When you get into the habit of putting off gratification, you'll begin to have no trouble at all getting started.

Don't start with email. This seems a bit odd at first glance. Sometimes the very first thing you do to start your morning is check your email to see if anyone wants anything from you. More often than not, the answer is yes; people always want something from you, and they want it yesterday. Well, that's the opposite of creating focus for yourself, isn't it? Understand your own priorities first and _then_ start on the emails.

Emails are a to-do list that other people have made for you. We don't realize this. But if something is important or urgent enough, people will make an effort to contact you in other ways, such as calling you or literally knocking on your door. And if it's not that important, eventually a non-response to an email will fade into irrelevancy. In other words, feel free to actually be _worse_ with email because others will compensate for it and the world will not fall apart. It's only hurting your focus.

Once you've done what you need to do for yourself, then you can start on what other people need from you and treat email as crossing something off *your* list. Emails have a magnetic quality about them that you need to avoid, lest you get sucked down rabbit hole after rabbit hole.

Start with the little things. It's hard to get motivated and maintain momentum when the first piece of work you do is one that will take hours, and can often not result in any significant feedback or progress. Imagine having your first task of the day be editing a gigantic, 30-page report. A bit discouraging, no?

Instead, break what you see in front of you into distinct, small tasks—ones you can do quickly so that you can immediately make visible progress. This way, you get the ball rolling as soon as you can, and you can keep up your motivation as you head for bigger and more challenging tasks. It's easy to get started when you can ease into warming up your brain, so to speak. More on this later.

Finally, aim to do as much as you can before noon. This could be different for other people, but when noon hits, I immediately think I'm over the halfway point of my day. Technically speaking, the day is half over, but I mean in terms of the allotment of my brain power. It's a massive psychological barrier. Noon means lunch is near, which leads to that inevitable period of time where you break your focus and must scramble to find your place afterwards. And of course, it's tough to recapture the mood.

By breaking momentum, you may never find it again that day, so do as much as you can in the morning hours when you're already in the zone before you have to take a break in the afternoon. Make it a competition—against yourself. After all, you're already an object in motion, so it shouldn't be a tough task.

It's hard enough to get through your daily tasks without being focused and in the right mindset. However, if you follow the wise words of Isaac Newton, you'll find that creating motion to begin your day means that you will be less likely to stop or slow down, and the work will be done before you know it.

#2. Productive Mornings

In the same vein as starting your days right is trying to adhere to a morning routine that will help battle your tendency to procrastinate.

Humans are creatures of habit and routine. In some order, you wake up, brush your teeth, sit on the porcelain throne, and get dressed.

Your morning sets the tone for your entire day, so what can you add to that morning routine that will jumpstart your day and let you focus on what you need to focus on?

We all know how easy it is to zone out in the morning and literally lose hours of your day by aimlessly browsing the internet. In the morning, because we're usually tired, it's too easy for the inertia of non-productivity to grab hold of us. Even if we're at work, sometimes it can take a couple of hours to get into the swing of the day's tasks and goals. It might be after lunch before you're feeling ready to dive into something big.

This is clearly what we're trying to avoid. How can you make your mornings more productive, have greater output, and have less procrastination? Create a productive morning routine for yourself.

Your best productivity starts when you have clearly defined goals. Why not have those goals and a proper mindset in place the minute you wake up? After you buy into the morning productivity routine, you'll find that it will become instinct for you to do productive acts when you wake up, which will transition naturally into accomplishing bigger and bigger tasks.

Instead of clicking aimlessly on random websites, you will gradually begin to click over to your tasks and action items.

What's on this morning's productivity routine? It's a fixed checklist that is specific in its sequence.

1. Wake up. Don't hit the snooze button. Don't you *dare*. We've covered this already.

2. Check the daily checklist you created the night before. Reviewing your list will immediately let you know what's on the docket for the day so you can start thinking about how to tackle it. Let it simmer in the back of your mind subconsciously as you go about the rest of your morning routine. It's a good idea to write these down by hand so you don't have to encounter your tempting phone. Five minutes.

3. NO SOCIAL MEDIA, NO EMAILS YET. Don't let these distractions cloud the priorities you carefully laid out the night before. These can also be incredibly distracting in the morning, so save what would otherwise be a wasted hour and leave the social media for a break later in the day. After all, there really isn't that much going on in the world that affects you on a day-to-day basis.

4. Bathroom routines—cleaning, grooming, relieving. It is many people's first urge to do this, but I implore you to reconsider. If you can program yourself to hold off on these essentials until after you look at your daily checklist, then the daily checklist becomes essential as well. Ruminate on your checklist while you're going through this part of your routine. When you plant the seeds of your checklist in your mind earlier and intentionally don't act on them immediately, you accomplish two underrated things.

First, you get to think about it and know that you don't need to deal with them at that instant—a bit of the pleasant feeling of procrastination. Second, you eventually become eager to do it because you've been thinking about it; you actually grow a sense of anticipation about it. 10 minutes.

5. Get started on something. It's key to do this before breakfast or coffee. You're seizing the anticipation you have built

up from looking at your daily checklist. Start it before sitting down to breakfast. The reason? Because this just might keep your breakfast short and focused in anticipation of you getting back to your task. Be preoccupied during your breakfast or coffee. Often, this will drive you to keep working on it during breakfast as well. Hopefully you can isolate a couple of smaller tasks to start your day with a couple of easy, encouraging wins. 20 minutes.

6. Breakfast or coffee. Make sure you already know what you're going to prepare so you don't waste time trying to cobble something together from the contents of your fridge! It's a good idea to have the same thing for breakfast every morning so you don't need to devote any brainpower to it. Whatever the case, prepare beforehand so you don't have to make a decision in the morning. Instead, reserve your mind for being preoccupied with what you started earlier. 15 minutes.

7. Check your emails. Yes, finally, check your emails and reply to the most urgent messages. I've waited until this point to include this because otherwise, you risk getting dangerously derailed from the other priorities you set the night before. You might have an urgent matter or two in there, but nothing that can't wait an hour. Sometimes we are beholden to others, but far less than we think. Just do what's necessary here, not a total overhaul of your inbox. 15 minutes.

8. Re-evaluate your daily checklist after seeing if there are any urgent matters in your emails. Five minutes.

9. Goof around. Indulge yourself a little bit to raise your mood for the upcoming productive day... but only after you've started the ball rolling on multiple fronts! This will naturally discourage you from goofing around, and you might even begin to skip this part of the routine. But still, this is necessary for most. 10 minutes.

As you can see, this morning routine will skyrocket your productivity by cutting the fat in your mornings and getting you right down to business. It sets the tone for the rest of your day.

When you are productive first thing in the morning, you'll end up producing a lot for the rest of the day. Don't let those opportunities pass you by. Mornings can be make-or-break in terms of your day's productivity, and which one they will be depends on whether you can seize the inherent momentum.

#3. Break It Up

I've touched on this already, but another one of the keys to kicking your butt into gear is to make your gears very easy to get going. In other words, make your barrier to starting as small as possible by breaking your tasks down.

Case in point: Very few people want to go to work when it's raining cats and dogs outside. It's an enormous burden to overcome mentally. You'll get soaked, your shoes and socks will be puddles, and you'll freeze from head to toe. Oh, and your only umbrella is broken. It's such a burden that you don't even want to go through the motions of getting dressed and putting on your boots. You feel defeated before you even get started, so you never do.

A horrendously rainy day can feel just like trying to be productive. When we're faced with huge tasks that feel insurmountable, it's like looking through your window out at the rain. It's such an obstacle that everything feels impossible and pointless. We drag our feet, discourage ourselves, and bitterly complain the whole time.

A single huge task, such as "finish the 200-page report," can certainly sound imposing, if not impossible. However, what if you were to break that monumental task up into tiny, individual, easy tasks that you can get to work on immediately? For example: preparing the template, finding the first three sources, creating a bibliography, outlining five hundred words of the first section, and so on.

Otherwise, you're starting each day staring at the task equivalent of a rainy day.

One of the biggest hurdles to productivity is looking at tasks as huge, inseparable boulders. It's intimidating and discouraging, and when those emotions arise, it's tough to avoid procrastinating because tackling a boulder is a tough sell. Unfortunately, this is a habit that plagues most people. They see only massive boulders and allow themselves to get emotionally thrown off-track.

Break up your big tasks into smaller tasks, and keep repeating until the tasks you have before you are so easy you can do them within a few minutes. Create small, manageable chunks that will be psychologically uplifting and acceptable, and you'll kick your production up instantly. Make your to-do list as long and articulated as possible with as many small tasks as you can list out.

Productivity is nothing without action, and action is much easier with something simple and easy to warm up with. Small steps can take you to the top of the hill and let you roll down the other side to seize momentum. They help you break the inertia that leads you to passivity and inaction.

When you can knock out any task in a matter of minutes, you create more confidence in yourself to tackle the bigger tasks. You feel more at ease, and your mind is imbued with the knowledge and confidence that you've already done quite a bit, so the rest won't be a problem.

Create small victories for yourself and think "manageable" and "immediate." Trying to wrap your mind around a boulder only freezes your mind up and creates analysis paralysis because you won't have any idea of where to start. When you look at the big stuff, your first thought is that it's too tough, impossible, or highly unpleasant. Small chunks are easy to visualize and imagine doing, which means half the battle is already won.

Let's take an example that we're all familiar with: working out. You want to lose 100 pounds, a hefty goal. If you go into the gym every day thinking that you want to lose 100 pounds, you're probably going to fail. It's a huge, enormous boulder of a goal. It might sound grand to proclaim, but in reality, it is going to be very hard to stick to because of how unbelievable it sounds.

You won't see much progress on a daily or even weekly basis, and you will understandably become discouraged. It's too much to face at once, like the rainy day from the beginning of the chapter.

What if you approached your weight loss goal by breaking it into small, manageable increments (goals) and tasks? This might look something like setting a reasonable weekly weight loss goal, creating daily goals of eating specific foods (and not eating others), and drinking water every hour. Eat 100 fewer calories per meal. Go on walks after each meal.

If you hit your weekly weight loss goal and successfully drink water every hour, it is far easier to stay motivated and focused. Meeting your smaller weekly goal will give you a sense of accomplishment, whereas making an insignificant dent in your total goal (100 pounds) will only make you feel discouraged and as if the task ahead is too great to achieve.

These are small tasks that, if done consistently and correctly, will lead you to achieving your overall goal of losing 100 pounds.

The emphasis here is on accomplishing small and immediate tasks and goals; these small victories will encourage and motivate you. Always seek to break your tasks up into smaller components, even if when the entire task is normal- or small-sized to begin with. Don't underestimate the power of small victories.

#4. "Don't-Do" List

Sometimes when we're struggling to get started, it's because we can't choose what to fixate on. Too many things have the potential to command our focus, and sometimes we can't differentiate between what we should avoid and what actually deserves our attention. Thus, the focus of this section is to make crystal clear what you should be getting started on.

Everyone knows the value of the to-do list. Even if you haven't read about it prior to this book, no doubt you've stumbled across tips elsewhere about using a to-do list to increase productivity.

My point is that everyone inherently *kind of* knows what they should be doing and when they need to do it by. The act of writing it down just helps remind them. This makes them more likely to do what they know they should be doing—more than if they didn't have such a list.

Granted, this is mostly common sense and not what you bought this book for. Well, here it is: not everyone knows what they *shouldn't* be doing. Along with your to-do list, it's equally important to make a *don't-*

do list. Each day, we're faced with choosing tasks that will create the biggest impact for us, and there are many hidden obstacles.

Again, we all know the obvious evils to avoid when trying to upgrade productivity: social media, goofing around on the internet, watching *The Bachelorette* while trying to work, or learning to play the flute while reading.

It can be difficult to distinguish between real tasks and useless tasks, and it will require some hard thought on your part.

You need to fill your don't-do list with tasks that will sneakily steal your time and undermine your goals. These are tasks that are insignificant or a poor use of your time, tasks that don't help your bottom line, and tasks that have a serious case of diminishing returns the more you work on them.

If you continuously devote and waste your time on these tasks, your real priorities and goals will be left untouched. Here's what you should put on your *don't*-do list:

First, tasks that are priorities, but you can't do anything about them at present because of external circumstances.

These are tasks that are important in one or many ways, but are waiting for feedback from others, or for underlying tasks to be completed first. Put these on your don't-do list because there is literally nothing you can do about them!

Don't spend your mental energy thinking about them. They'll still be there when you hear back from those other people. Just note that you are waiting to hear back from someone else and the date on which you need to follow-up if you haven't heard back. Then push these out of your mind, because they're on someone else's to-do list, not yours.

You can also temporarily push things off your plate by clarifying and asking questions of other people. This puts the ball in their court to act, and you can take that time to catch up on other matters.

Second are tasks that don't add value as far as your projects are concerned.

There are many small items that don't add to your bottom line, and often, these are trivial things—busywork. Can you delegate these, assign them to someone else, or even outsource them? Do they really require your time? In other words, are they *worth* your time? And will anyone but you notice the difference if you delegate the task to someone else? By taking on the task yourself, are you getting stuck in the weeds of perfectionism? These tasks are just wasted motion for the sake of motion and don't really matter in the big picture.

You should spend your time on big tasks that move entire projects forward and not myopic, trivial tasks. Often, these are useless tasks disguised as important ones, such as selecting the paint color for the bike shed in the parking lot of the nuclear power plant you are building.

Third, include tasks that are current and ongoing, but will not benefit from additional work or attention paid to them. These tasks suffer from diminishing returns.

These tasks are just a waste of energy because while they can still stand to improve (and is there anything that can't?), the amount of likely improvement will either not make a difference in the overall outcome or success, or will take a disproportionate amount of time and effort without making a significant dent.

For all intents and purposes, these tasks should be considered *done*. Don't waste your time on them, and don't fall into the trap of considering them a priority. Once you finish everything else on your plate, you can then evaluate how much time you want to devote to polishing something.

If the task is at 90% of the quality you need it to be, it's time to look around at what else needs your attention to bring it from 0% to

90%. In other words, it's far more helpful to have three tasks completed at 80% quality versus one task at 100% quality.

When you consciously avoid the items on your don't-do list, you keep yourself focused and streamlined. You don't waste energy or time, and your daily output will increase dramatically.

Why read a menu with food items that are unavailable? It's pointless. By preventing your energy level from being dissipated by those things that suck up your time and attention, a don't-do list enables you to take care of the important stuff first.

The fewer things that tug on your mind, the better—the kind of stress and anxiety they create only hampers or kills productivity. A don't-do list will free your mind from the burden of having too many things in the air because it eliminates most of those things! You can focus on the balls that are still in flight and steadily knock each one out.

#5. Reward Yourself

I'm always amazed when I watch videos of dogs that can perform countless tricks.

How were their owners able to train them so effectively? Are dogs smarter than we think? Are they truly man's best friend? Yes and no. Their owners reward them with enough treats to make them fat. They bribe them with rewards that motivate them into action.

A dog will bend over backwards, crawl through mud, leap through hoops, walk on two legs, do flips, and run obstacle courses if you make it clear you will be rewarding them properly afterward. Dogs become highly motivated and focused when they know something they want is at stake.

Imagine a rabbit with a carrot tied in front of him. The rabbit can't reach the carrot, but he keeps running faster and faster to get a bite of his favorite food.

We're not much different from animals. We function and focus far better if we have a clear goal and reward to work for. For the most part, if we choose our reward intelligently enough, it can lure us into action much sooner than we would even prefer, or be ready for. Just picture when you're exhausted and sleep-deprived, but hear the familiar jingle of the ice cream truck growing louder. You might just draw yourself up and outside. Rewards get results.

Humans are creatures of incentives, and this is undeniable when we look at our daily actions. Everything we have and do is a reflection of the incentives we have and the reward we work toward. Whether our incentive is food, sex, social status, or money, we are driven by a perceived benefit or reward.

Knowing this, we can boost our daily productivity and spring into action by setting rewards for ourselves to keep us focused. If we do it properly, we can program ourselves to achieve amazing levels of productivity with simple rewards.

The first step is to define the rewards that will actually motivate you into action. You can also frame them as punishments. If you don't finish the task at hand, will you:

- Not get a snack?
- Not book your trip to Italy?
- Not get Chinese for dinner?
- Not hang out with that cutie tonight?
- Not buy that shirt for yourself?

For our purposes of getting started, we want to pair getting into action with something correspondingly quick and instant as a reward. This means we're probably looking at mostly short-term rewards, like rewarding yourself with chocolate the way a dog gets a treat for a trick.

This may not work for everyone, but the way that worked for me was literally stockpiling bags of chocolates so I could reward myself every time I had to use my willpower to get started and into action. I had them on-hand for a couple of weeks, and two patterns began to emerge.

First, it motivated me to action because I knew there was something pleasurable after engaging in the unpleasurable. This was predictable. Second, I actually began to associate the process and act of getting started with... pleasure. Just like Pavlov and his dog, I had become the dog who was able to create a positive association with breaking through my inertia, despite it being an innately uncomfortable act. I was able to condition myself. This may not occur with everyone, but it's certainly a possibility, given that our drives don't work much differently than a dog's.

Rewards can also come in the long-term form; they may not be so tangibly motivating and impactful, but they can push people into action because they begin to understand what's at stake.

For instance, put a picture of Italy or Hawaii up right by your desk so you are constantly reminded of what you're working toward and can positively motivate yourself, knowing you will only buy your plane tickets if you hit certain milestones you set.

When you associate putting in the necessary amount of work with your reward, you take away the stigma of tedious work and slowly associate it with a happy ending.

When you use immediate, short-term goals in conjunction with overarching, long-term goals, you'll find more reasons than not to jump into action. Sometimes we just need a reminder to nudge us to take that first step.

There's a reason they call it work. I don't care whether you are a lawyer, a doctor, an accountant, or a dog trainer, certain parts of every job and task are a drag. When you use the power of conditioning yourself through rewards, you short-circuit this negative association, and the work becomes a means to a desired end.

In the end, it all boils down to what motivates you and having a clear view of what you're putting in all your work for. If you don't know what you're working for, then why would you work hard at all? It's like working at a job where you get the same compensation regardless of how hard you work. You go through the motions without direction or interest.

If your effort isn't tied to something that keeps you motivated, then why make an effort at all?

Takeaways:

- Focus is tough, but the toughest part about focus is simply getting started. It's because we all have to deal with a certain amount of inertia to begin our days. Getting into motion from a standstill takes energy, but there are ways to short-circuit the process for yourself.
- First, take note of Newton's law of momentum. This states that when an object is in motion, it tends to stay in motion, and when an object is at rest, it tends to stay at rest. How can you be an object that stays in motion? It starts with how you wake up, begin your day, and don't allow time for inertia to set in.
- Productive mornings go hand in hand with Newton's law. When you can create

a galvanizing and energizing morning routine for yourself, you can set the tone you want for the rest of the day. The morning routine that is recommended leaves little to no room for decisions or thought, and depends on planting the seeds of your tasks so you grow anticipation toward them.

- Getting started is easier when you have something small and easy in front of you. After all, it is easier to take a single step versus climb a mountain, even though they both have the same end goal. Therefore, break all of your tasks into smaller sub-tasks, and then do it again. This psychologically makes it easy for you to get started and take action.

- We all know what we should do, roughly speaking. But it's those things that we shouldn't do that sometimes keep us from getting started. We should avoid the sneaky tasks that are secret wastes of time. This should all be encapsulated in a "don't-do" list, where you make sure to note things to ignore and not pay attention to because they would distract you from what actually matters.

- Finally, motivate yourself into action with rewards. Make sure to use short-term rewards to instantly provide yourself with pleasure after getting started. Pair this with long-term goals that keep you motivated on a deeper level. Both of these have the pleasant side effect of taking the stigma away from your work and creating a positive and happy association with it.

Section 2. Create and Seize Momentum

Now that you've gotten off your butt and into action, everything will be smooth sailing, right?

Yes, in a world where we are all millionaires and ride tigers as our main form of transportation. In other words, no; while just getting started is the most difficult part, that doesn't mean it's the *only* part of gaining focus and launching into productivity.

Once you've gotten started, you're in a delicate stage where you have to protect your focus to make sure that you properly create momentum for yourself. Otherwise, you'll sink back to inaction—and if you thought getting into motion the first time was difficult, the second time will prove to be near-impossible.

To borrow from another field, think about how daunting and difficult it is to walk up to an attractive member of the opposite sex and introduce yourself. Yet, it is the words directly after the introduction that matter the most and determine how the interaction will ultimately go, despite the fact that the introduction was more difficult. This section is focused on how to pick up steam and turn into a focused productivity machine.

#6. Kill Perfectionism

Perfectionism is one of the most important beasts you'll have to slay to create and maintain momentum. Perfection taken to an extreme degree has another name: Obsessive-compulsive disorder (OCD).

Yes, your perfectionism can be similarly unhealthy and damaging to your focus and productivity.

If you have to lock and unlock your doors five times before you can leave your house, it's no different than editing a document for the fifth and unnecessary time. It prevents you from doing what you want in a timely manner, all in the name of making sure something is picture perfect. When we look at someone with OCD who's struggling with their tendencies, all we see is unnecessary motion for no real reason. Perfectionism in regard to your work will similarly keep you paralyzed.

Defeating your perfectionist tendencies is one of the best things you can do to remain in motion and create momentum. This is because, almost universally, what's more important is what you actually follow through with something, not that something is flawless. It's far better to bring 100 cookies to a bake sale than 20 perfectly iced cookies. And it's *far, far* better to perform three surgeries to adequate completion rather than perform one surgery to precise perfection. Perfection is not what makes the world go 'round.

In every area of life, perfection is not expected, and there are always buffers for a margin of error. Did you know that in preserved goods, there is an acceptable amount of insects that might be mixed in? Sometimes disgustingly, we can't create perfection, and rarely does it ever make a difference.

In your personal life, because everyone makes mistakes of their own, a lack of perfection is almost always excusable. Everyone knows they make mistakes too, and they are in no position to judge you for something that isn't perfect. Everyone hits their own snags from time to time.

That's the first realization you must have to destroy perfectionism. Knowing that people accept imperfection is a big part of the mindset that will smash through your inertia and help you take your first steps. Your internal standards may be high, and you may be your own harshest critic, but the rest of the world does not operate on that rubric. It doesn't benefit anyone else in any tangible way, and it keeps you in a prison of your own making. Who are your perfectionist tendencies really serving? Only you, your fears, and your insecurities. That leads to the second realization.

The second realization is that perfectionist tendencies typically manifest to protect ego and pride—to make sure you are as rejection-proof as possible, and to prevent a hit to your self-esteem.

For the most part, perfectionists are not necessarily driven by a need for excellence—they are really people who are petrified by judgment. They feel that any error on their part will reflect poorly on them as a whole, and people will cast judgment on their intellect or character. Thus, they leave as little to chance as possible by *perfecting* it.

To illustrate, think of the last time you praised an artistic friend's painting. Imagine that they were highly reluctant to show it to you because they felt that they drew a hand poorly. You surely can't tell, because to you the painted hand looks perfectly hand-like. You couldn't tell the difference between what you were seeing in the painting and your friend's standard of perfection. It made no difference to you whatsoever.

However, to your friend, they saw every little mistake and assumed that everyone else could as well. They fixated on the negative judgments the hand would create about them as a person, and thus kept working on the hand to the detriment of finishing the actual painting.

Your output is severely hampered when you waste time trying to *"get everything right."* Instead of producing fully, which the job or social situation might call for, you'll only produce a tiny fraction of what was expected or requested.

Often, this tiny fraction is useless by itself, so you have just left a job incomplete by giving in to your perfectionist tendencies. What good are five perfectly decorated cupcakes when you were supposed to bring 20? Who wins in that situation? Certainly not the 15 people who didn't get a cupcake, with or without sprinkles! And certainly not you.

Perfectionism slows you down. By always looking back and double- and triple-checking your work, you are going to be moving at a snail's pace. At best, you produce a mere portion of what you should, and at worst, you are completely paralyzed by "analysis paralysis" and produce absolutely nothing.

Let's be clear that minimum standards do exist. You can't expect to succeed with low-quality writing, for example, but a cost-benefit analysis must often be done to see what the optimal pairing of standards and speed is.

Perfectionism also destroys momentum, which is an *everyday superpower* that should be leveraged for maximum productivity and output. When you can't let go of your perfectionism, you bring your momentum to a screeching halt. And it takes a tremendous amount of energy to get it going again.

In this sense, perfectionism is procrastination because it allows you to avoid future steps. Instead of forging forward, you might always be looking over your shoulder.

Being *"in the zone"* is the sense of momentum, and that's almost certainly a result of letting go of perfectionism. It's when ideas are flowing from your brain to your hands or your keyboard and you aren't even thinking—you are acting. Not everything you're doing is going to be perfect in that zone, but it doesn't matter, because you just need to keep translating your thoughts into work or words.

Staying in perfectionist mode is incredibly inefficient. By definition, you are overly focused on getting every little detail correct. This means you're probably focusing on the *wrong* details while larger issues are lurking and waiting for your attention. It's a very easy trap to fall into, and even easier to get blindsided by.

It's not an easy thing to let go of, but attempt to focus on maximizing your output and on the bigger picture—because that's the real issue with perfectionists. They get caught up in the trees and lose sight of the forest, where the forest is the big picture goal they are working toward. Just realize there are diminishing returns on perfection while the big picture goal will still be sitting there, waiting.

First things first: Finish what you need, then invest more time in quality and performance. This leads directly to the next point.

#7. Edit Later

There are a lot of sayings about writers and their profession.

The road to hell is paved with works-in-progress.

It ain't what you write, it's how you write it.

We are all apprentices in a craft where no one ever becomes a master.

And finally, my favorite:

Write drunk, edit sober.

But my second favorite, and the focus of this point, is this one:

Write first, edit later.

The overarching message is that you should finish everything you're writing (or doing, whatever your task may be) before you double-check and spend time editing and revising it. Don't become distracted by backtracking and killing your momentum. Keep moving forward until you finish. This doesn't only apply to writers, though writing and writers are a helpful illustration.

If you're a writer and you try to make every word choice and phrase perfect, you'll probably be writing at the snail's pace of one page a day. But guess what? Your perfect prose isn't the reason people will be compelled to buy your book. And moreover, there *won't be a book to buy* if you write so slowly, get mired in the details, and don't ever complete the manuscript.

So what's the point? *Do first, edit later*. This is a tactic that will skyrocket your productivity and momentum because it encourages you to push forward and get everything you can onto the page before getting bogged down by small details (and before some of your best ideas slip away while you're focusing on perfecting a sentence). Stay on target with the big picture goal and leave the details for when you have extra time.

It also encourages the maxim of *do first, think later*, which you will benefit from as well. Stop thinking and plotting before you put pen to paper and simply start writing. You'll get into the swing when you start doing it and find your momentum building. For writers, this means to start typing whatever comes to mind and let it eventually get around to what you originally intended to write about. You'll have more material to play with in the end anyway.

The simple truth with most tasks in our daily life is that having all of *something* is far more important than having 75%_of something that has been edited to perfection. Having an entire task, batch, or paper done is always the primary goal. Don't lose sight of that by spending time tightening up your work before you have everything you need. Completion is the goal.

Too many people mistake a well-edited task for productivity.

Here's a dose of reality: that's not what you're paid to do. You're getting paid for how much work you complete. A completed checklist has far more value than a well-edited fraction of that list.

The overarching principle behind this productivity tip is that you need to take action *now* and focus on reflection later when you have the luxury of time. You are in a race against the clock, whether you realize it or not. Capitalize on the momentum you have, finish what you have to finish, and *then* reflect on what you've done when you can look at all of it. This is where you can edit and polish. What's important is that you get everything out of the way and taken care of before you start tightening things up and perfecting them. That's what you do when you've completed your task.

If you're so focused on whipping everything into shape, it will take you a very long time to produce very little work. The world rewards productivity and results, not the effort or the process. There are no prizes for "almost" or second place.

I would even go so far as to say that output and productivity comes first and quality comes second. I'm not saying you should abandon the idea of producing quality work. However, you should put things in proper perspective and understand that *producing* comes first.

No book (task) = no money (payoff), no matter how beautiful your prose and vocabulary are.

Within the details, there are those that matter and those that simply do not. Sometimes you will get your best results by ignoring some details that aren't significant and just focusing on seeing through bigger tasks to completion.

Ship things out. Take care of business. Get it done. Make it so. Later, once you've finished what you need to finish, you can come back and increase the overall quality of the tasks you have completed. Momentum will come.

#8. Batch Tasks

Henry Ford, founder of Ford Motor Company, got a lot of things right about cars. He had a few competitors back in the day, but a primary reason those names are essentially lost in time is because he also the creator of the *factory assembly line*.

On a factory assembly line, workers focus on one task at a time.

This streamlines a process and makes it far more efficient than having a single worker see a project through from start to finish, switching between multiple tasks. It allows workers to specialize and perfect their task, which cuts down on errors and makes troubleshooting far easier. Workers didn't have to do more thinking than was necessary for the task at hand. For Ford, this made his automobile production efficiency and output shoot through the roof and dominate the market.

That, in essence, is what *batching* can do for you. It allows you to keep momentum instead of switching from task to task, interrupting your train of thought and having to start over constantly.

Batching is when you group similar tasks together to complete them all at once, or closely following each other. Ford's assembly line was essentially 100%

batching because his workers only performed one task incredibly efficiently.

Let's take a common example we can all relate to—checking your email inbox.

If you have any sort of online presence or job, you probably have a steady stream of emails trickling (or gushing) into your inbox every hour. Constantly checking your email is an extremely inefficient use of time. It interrupts other tasks and scatters your focus whenever you receive a new email. Many of us drop what we're doing to take care of something from an email. Then we have to start the original task over again because our flow and momentum has been interrupted.

Batching emails will considerably improve your productivity. An example of this would be to only check your emails at the top of every two hours and purposely ignore or block your inbox notifications. At first it might be difficult, but limiting how often you check email in this way allows you to focus on your tasks without constantly being distracted and having to re-acclimate yourself.

Perhaps more importantly, it teaches the lesson that saying "no" to some tasks is just as important as saying "yes" to the correct ones. Batching teaches the art of purposeful, deliberate ignorance so you can focus on other tasks. Imagine using this in conjunction with a "don't-do" list.

Switching from task to task is a large mental burden because you are stopping and starting from zero numerous times throughout the day. It takes energy to switch from task to task, and there are usually a few minutes wasted on regaining your bearings and figuring out the status of the task you were working on. Of course, these kinds of interruptions only lead to achieving just a portion of what you can and want to.

In the example of checking your emails, batching allows you to stay in a mindset of reading and composing emails with all its associated skills, tasks, and reminders.

Email catch-up is a distinctly different mode than designing a new graphic for an advertising campaign.

What else can you batch? You can schedule all your meetings for one afternoon so you will have a free, uninterrupted morning to work. You can plan to do everything that requires computer access in the morning, and even batch parts of tasks such as those which require you to make phone calls. Just categorize your tasks and put everything similar together to maintain better focus and momentum.

You can also batch your *distractions*.

This isn't to distract and amuse yourself more efficiently. It's to make sure that you are conserving your energy and allowing your focused time to be exactly that— focused.

How can you batch distractions? For example, if you're burned out on a particular task, you might want to take a little social media break. By all means, take it! However, allot just a bit more time to check *all* of your accounts—ESPN, Refinery29, and whatever other distractions you occupy yourself with. Grab a new cup of coffee, take a brisk walk around the office, and say hello to your neighbor.

Get it all out of your system so that when you're back to work, you can have a solid and fixed block of time in which to focus. After all, if there is nothing new on your Facebook page, you will probably feel less compelled to check it. Once you knock yourself out doing all these distracting activities within the allotted time, you can switch to productive work for the rest of your hour. What's important is that you are taking a *planned* break versus an *unplanned* break.

Some have referred to this as the *Pomodoro Technique.* A Pomodoro is a 30-minute block of time.

25 minutes of that time will be allotted to focused, hard work, while the remaining

five minutes will be a break. Once you complete four Pomodoros, you are allotted a 20-minute break. It works the same way as batching distractions, and it keeps you focused because you know you will have a reward distraction at the end of the work period. It might even drive you to finish as much as possible before your break.

The more you divide your attention among different activities, the less focused you'll be. When you begin doing something similar to the previous activity, you'll find it's much easier to get going because your mind is already geared toward doing a certain kind of task. Do all the similar tasks together, one after the other, and then move on to the next batch of similar or related activities. Effective batching can skyrocket your productivity no matter the context.

One of the biggest benefits of batching is that it prevents multitasking. Speaking of which...

#9. Single-tasking

Who would be great at multitasking? An octopus with two heads. As in, to multitask effectively, one literally needs two brains and eight hands. Guess how many brains and hands we are short? It's just not within human capability to multitask effectively, no matter what you think or have been told.

Multitasking is a big, fat lie. You simply can't do more than one thing efficiently at a time, so don't try to split your minutes in different directions. You can either do one thing well, or you can do three things very poorly. Unfortunately, too many people believe in it, overestimate themselves, and suffer lousy productivity as a result.

The main reason multitasking is so appealing to so many people is that they have inflated views of their capabilities. Most people believe they're good at many things, including the mental clarity to constantly switch between tasks from minute to minute. There's a sense of denial regarding the need for setting time aside and truly focusing.

In reality, it's like speed dating—you only get to know each task a little bit, and you don't really have enough information to make good judgment calls. There is no sense of familiarity with the time you're given and you end up with similarly ineffectual results. Everyone thinks they can do it, but there is a big difference between watching television while eating a sandwich and completing two tasks which require thought and effort at once. No one can do it well, even if they think they can, and trying to do it at all will only make you lose focus and end up performing worse at everything.

Let's take Bob. Bob is on the phone, on his tablet, and on a computer. He gets an email that seems urgent, so he starts to answer it while he's still talking on the phone. He completely loses track of the phone conversation, and the report he pulled up on his computer will have to be completely re-read to be understood. It only took one call or email to completely throw Bob off-track and for all of the things he was juggling to fall out of the air and land on his head.

By multitasking, the only thing that you will achieve is that you will end up continually distracting yourself, because your mind is focused on too many things to process them all equally and efficiently. According to a study in the *New York Times*, it can take up to 25 minutes to regain focus after being distracted. That's 25 minutes you will waste trying to find your place and get into the right mindset again.

In 2009, Sophie Leroy published a paper that was aptly titled "Why is it So Hard to Do My Work?" In it, she explained an effect that she called "attention residue."

Leroy noted that other researchers had studied the effect of multitasking on performance, but that in the modern work environment, once you reached a high enough level, it was more common to find people working on multiple projects sequentially. "Going from one meeting to the next, starting to work on one project and soon after having to transition to another is just part of life in organizations," Leroy explains.

This is essentially the modern version of multitasking—working on projects in short bursts and switching between them, not necessarily doing them all at once. People may not actually be working on multiple tasks at the same time, but it's nearly as bad to keep switching between them in relatively quick succession. For all intents and purposes, this is modern multitasking.

The problem identified by this research is that you cannot switch seamlessly between tasks without a delay of sorts. When you switch from Task A to Task B, your attention doesn't immediately follow—a residue of your attention remains stuck thinking about the original task. This becomes worse, and the residue becomes especially "thick" if your work on Task A was unbounded and of low intensity before you switched, but even if you finish Task A before moving on, your attention remains divided for a while.

Leroy's tests forced people to switch between different tasks in a laboratory setting. In one of these experiments, she assigned the subjects a set of word puzzles to work on. In one of the trials, she would interrupt their work and force them to move on to a new and challenging task—for example, reading resumes and making hypothetical hiring decisions. In other trials, she let the subjects finish the puzzles before giving them the next task.

While the participants were switching between puzzling and hiring, Leroy would play a quick lexical decision game. This was so she could quantify the amount of leftover residue from the first task. The results were clear: "People experiencing attention residue after switching tasks are likely to demonstrate poor performance on that next task," and the more intense the residue, the worse the performance.

This doesn't seem too far of a stretch when you think about it. We've all experienced that frantic moment when we're doing too many things at once and suddenly find ourselves unable to do any at all. How can you concentrate on any task if you keep switching back and forth between two or more different things? You'll likely be stuck simply trying to make sense of everything and organize it so you can understand it. It will only force you to waste time trying to catch up to where you were instead of pushing forward. You'll take one step forward, but two steps back each time you try.

Multitasking may seem to be the best of both worlds, but when you're in situations where there are multiple sources of information coming from the external world or emerging from memory, you cannot filter out what is irrelevant to your current goal. This failure to filter means that you are slowed down by irrelevant information and will struggle to complete a task without distractions. It is much easier to focus on one thing at once, without letting distractions interfere, than to try doing several things at a time and overloading your brain with too much information.

There might be certain ways you can multitask 1% more effectively, but the overall lesson is just to avoid it whenever possible. The answer is in the name of the point: single-tasking. What does this mean?

To set everything else aside and not check, monitor, email, or even touch anything other than the current task you are working on. It requires singular focus and the purposeful and intentional tuning out of everything else. Switch off your notifications and ditch your phone. If you must be on your computer, keep only one browser tab or program open at a time. Put yourself into a vacuum; if you grow bored or want to procrastinate, there's only one thing for you to do to exit the vacuum.

A lot of single-tasking is about consciously avoiding distractions that seem small and harmless. The biggest culprits? Your electronic devices. Ignore them when possible. Keep a spotless workspace so your eye doesn't catch something that needs cleaning or adjusting. Ideally, single-tasking reduces your environment to a blank room because you shouldn't pay attention to any of it. Out of sight, out of mind.

Attempt to pay attention to when you are being interrupted or subtly switching between tasks. This is hard to catch at first and will require you to make conscious decisions against your instincts.

Something that will be very hard to resist is the compulsion to tell yourself that you must act on something immediately and interrupt your task. However, don't confuse urgent with important. Matters, and people alike, all want to masquerade as important.

To combat this urge, set aside a notebook to take notes for ideas that will inevitably spring to mind regarding other tasks. Call this your *distraction list*. Just jot them down quickly and return to your primary goal. Whatever they're about, whether it's something that needs to be taken care, or something new and creative that pops into your head, take note, but don't act on them right when they come. Don't chase random thoughts, which are the equivalent of shiny objects.

Some of these might make their way into your to-do list, but most will probably end up on the "don't-do" list. You can address them after your single-tasking period is over, and you won't have forgotten anything. It will keep your mind focused on one single task while setting you up for future success.

Get in the habit of taking notes in general— this simple act frees up your brain for the present moment and doesn't let the future or the past interfere. Great ideas come in a flash and are gone the next second.

A big part of focus is organizing your thoughts and ideas so you can remember them and efficiently implement them at a later time. If you fail to capture your ideas at the moment they present themselves, chances are great you will forget them and lose out on the potential flood of increased productivity.

Our memories are pretty unreliable; in fact, studies show that eyewitness reports from memory are a terrible source of evidence in criminal trials.

Write everything down, even if you think it's not going to be important. Chances are what you write down will be a thread that leads to another thread that may just lead to the answer you have been seeking for weeks. Maximize your focus by keeping yourself rooted in the present, but also set yourself up for future success through your writings.

When you're in the thick of a busy day, your mind doesn't turn off. Keep a running log of everything you write down with you at all times. You might be surprised at the small things that used to fall through the cracks in your life. It might be as simple as remembering to buy more milk, or as important as a key creative idea that may generate thousands of dollars for you.

The solutions to your problems can come to you in an instant. It would be a shame if you're not properly equipped to record these solutions. There's literally no cost to you—just the effort involved in cultivating a habit that *all* of history's greatest thinkers have practiced and excelled at.

#10. Distraction Blackouts

If you've ever lost your Wi-Fi connection while working, you know it was one of the most productive days of your life.

Without Wi-Fi, you couldn't check Facebook, Twitter, ESPN, Snapchat, Reddit, Instagram—you couldn't even watch Netflix! In other words, you couldn't access any of your most beloved distractions, and when the boredom set in, you actually had no choice but to focus on what you wanted to avoid.

You probably also completed it in record time. When we're faced with the choice of sitting and doing nothing for hours or focusing, we're always going to choose to focus.

In the past, you had unintentional *distraction blackouts*—a forced period of time where you have no choice but to ignore all your usual distractions. It's obvious that this will lead to high productivity and focus, so let's make it a habit to regularly schedule distraction blackouts.

All you need to do is block out an entire afternoon—at least two, but no more than four hours—and deprive yourself of any other distractions so you are literally forced to work on a task. Turn your phone on silent (actually, turn it off and leave it at home), turn your Wi-Fi off, don't rearrange your desk or office, and don't you dare procrastinate otherwise. Sit in an empty room with a single desk and chair, if you have to. Some people wear earplugs.

Gather only what you need to occupy yourself for the next two to four hours, and nothing else that you would find interesting whatsoever. The point of the distraction blackout is to force you into a zone where you have no choice but to work. I know it's hard; you are forcing yourself into an uncomfortable situation for the greater good.

You are put in a position where you have two choices: to sit staring blankly and stupidly, wasting time, or to begrudgingly do something productive. It's the ultimate *I might as well* situation.

Once you're in the blackout, you can ramp up your productivity by competing against yourself.

Make it a game of accomplishment by measuring your output at the top of every hour. Competition is one of the most motivating factors, no matter who you are competing with, because your pride is on the line.

You are racing against the clock and yourself. Work is not inherently motivating, so let's say you plan to edit 20,000 words during a blackout. If you only edited 5,000 words the first hour, you'd better do at least

6,500 the next hour. Whatever you accomplished in the first hour (or day, or distraction blackout), try to top yourself in the next period. This will prove surprisingly addicting and ramp up your efficiency.

Make sure your list of objectives for that blackout is longer than you think you might be able to complete. If your blackout is going to be three hours, include what you think would amount to five hours of work. The reality is that what could be five hours of work *outside* a blackout may really only be three hours of distraction-free work. You'll be surprised what you can accomplish when you are in the zone. Create this game plan before the fact so you can reach for the next task as you finish your current one.

Finally, you should schedule your distraction blackouts for your most productive timeframe of the day.

You might notice that some parts of your day are always more productive than others. Some of us are night owls while others are morning birds. Most people naturally have peak performance hours when they are more alert and sharp, no matter what the context. As a result, the work we produce is better and needs less editing during those periods.

For example, my optimal time to schedule a distraction blackout is late afternoon or after dinner. I simply function better later in the day, and perhaps don't fully wake up until then. It doesn't matter what I've done during the day before that period of time; I can produce more at 50% mental capacity during those time periods than 100% mental capacity earlier in the day, most of the time.

Figuring out your peak productivity hours and combining them with distraction blackouts is a productivity double whammy. You'll be exponentially focused and alert if you pair them together, and knock out tasks on your lists at a rate you've never worked at before.

Regardless of how long your peak productivity times are and where they occur, during your day, you need to take advantage of them. You don't want to waste this highly productive "sweet spot" playing video games or answering emails. Talk about wasted resources! Instead, plan for maximum productivity during these times.

There is an extra benefit to a distraction blackout, and that is the level of deep thought you are able to devote to a single subject or topic. You're able to think about it beyond the primary concerns you normally only see in passing, and can think at the secondary and tertiary levels. You'll be able to visualize all the connections between topics and tasks in a new light, and your creativity will be awakened. I frequently come up with spontaneous ideas for improvements, new projects, and exploring things I'm thinking about, or working on more deeply during a distraction blackout.

You aren't able to truly delve into a topic if you are constantly distracted. You'll understand the surface level, but only sitting, fixating, and focusing for extended periods of time will provide the sorts of insights and realizations that will move the needle for you.

Takeaways:

- Momentum is a delicate thing. While the first section was focused on getting started, this section is on step two, three, and four, and making sure you capitalize on your hot start. Momentum by itself may be easier to achieve than breaking inertia, but it can slip away in just a moment.
- An easy way for momentum to slip away is through perfectionist tendencies. Perfectionism is nitpicking at every small detail at the detriment of overall progress. It emphasizes quality over quantity—this by itself isn't negative, but all things in moderation. To boot, the main reason most people engage in perfectionism isn't because of an adherence to excellence—it is because of fear of judgment and rejection.

- Perfectionism will halt you in your steps. So will constantly doubling back and editing, correcting, and tweaking things before you finish 100% of something. Do and complete first, edit later. This doesn't just apply to writing. When you go back to fix or change something, you lose your train of thought and cease to keep going forward. You begin to slide backwards, and by the time you finish editing, you've taken one step forward and two steps back. Completion is almost always your real goal.

- Multitasking is a myth. We've all heard this, but it's time to hear it again. We know that trying to work on several things simultaneously just results in poor quality across the board—most of us avoid this, at this point. However, we still tend to switch between tasks frequently, which is the modern version of multitasking. It takes far longer than you might expect to shrug off a distraction and return to your previous mental state, so defeat multitasking by single-tasking and focusing. If you feel that you need to address something during your single-tasking period, just write it on a distractions list and don't confuse something that's urgent for something that's important.

- Get in the habit of taking notes in general—this simple act frees up your brain for the present moment and doesn't let the future or the past interfere.
- Finally, distraction blackouts can increase your momentum because they force you into a state of boredom and isolation. When you're bored, you have a choice to remain bored, or begrudgingly work on what's in front of you. Intentionally put yourself into an uncomfortable situation, and you'll come out the other side in a better position. Use competition against yourself as an additional motivator. Make sure to schedule a distraction blackout during your time of greatest daily energy and efficiency.

Section 3. How to Stay Focused

Have you ever gone surfing?

Surfing generally has three phases. First is when you pop up onto your board from a lying position. This is difficult and requires a fantastic amount of balance. Second is when you transition from lying down into a stable standing position. Third is when you make your position stable for however long the wave you're riding is going to last.

It matches up quite well with our approach to focus and productivity. The hardest part was just getting started, and we just learned a bit about how to transition into a phase of momentum. Now we are looking for ways to solidify our focus and either reach "the zone" or stay in it.

For the third phase of relentless focus, we need to look beyond obvious methods and get resourceful. This section is about setting yourself up for success, whereas the prior section was about simply avoiding pitfalls.

#11. Your Circadian Rhythm

Your *circadian rhythm* is the cycle your energy levels go through on a daily basis. Why does this matter to your sense of focus and productivity?

Sleep researcher Neil Kleitman discovered that the body generally operates in 90-minute cycles, moving progressively through periods of higher and lower alertness. Understanding the circadian rhythm can help us predict how a person might function during a typical 24-hour period. The sequence applies whether we are awake or asleep, and we can use this information to our advantage by scheduling tasks to coincide with our own peak performance times.

In other words, we're wired to work and focus in 90-minute blocks; any less and you might be wasting your energy, but more and you might risk burning out.

As we move through a typical day, it takes a few hours after waking to reach our peak levels of energy and alertness. For most people, the late morning hours after 10:00 a.m. represent their highest period of mental clarity. This is the best time to begin tasks that require heavy cognitive input—like scheduling, mathematical equations, or persuasive writing. It's generally a good idea to match the difficulty of a task with your energy and alertness level.

Focusing on intense tasks during the late morning hours takes advantage of your fully awake brain, increasing productivity by syncing with your natural rhythm. Tony Schwartz, writing for the *Harvard Business Review*, reports that Kleitman found that working intensely for 90 minutes, followed by a rest period of no more than 15–20 minutes, is the ideal sequence for optimum mental performance. This follows the rhythm we see in sleep.

According to Schwartz, at the end of an intense 90-minute work period, we begin relying on stress hormones for energy. Suffering from overload, the prefrontal cortex begins to shut down and we move into fight-or-flight syndrome. We may attempt to override the body's signals by fueling ourselves with caffeine and sugar, which buys us a little more productive work time, but in the end, our focus and concentration still suffer. This might work in the short-term, but can be detrimental on an extended basis.

The point here is to listen to your body. It is telling you exactly how it prefers to function during sleep, and it is no different when awake. When you sit down to work, you are a ticking time bomb set for 90 minutes, after which you lose peak effectiveness and focus. Of course, some people may be less or more talented in this field, but your focus isn't limitless. This is also why it's so important to get rid of distractions so they are not allowed to eat into your 90-minute period of peak performance.

Time is finite, but our energy levels are far more finite. We only have a finite amount of energy each day during which we can produce great work, so we must not let it go to waste.

What works for others won't necessarily work for you. Don't try to be someone you're not when your intuition tells you that mornings aren't for you. While many people have powerful morning routines, you might not fully wake up until 2:00 p.m. or later.

#12. Chewing and Eating

How can something as easy as chewing gum help you improve your focus? Well, research conducted by the *British Journal of Psychology* shows that chewing gum increases the oxygen flow to certain parts of your brain that are responsible for your attention span—the prefrontal cortex, which resides over what are generally known as *executive functions*. This extra oxygen means that you will be more alert, and your reflexes will improve as well.

Seem too good to be true? Well, there's more. The increased blood flow also improves your long-term memory so that you are able to store and recall more information. This is very helpful when you are trying to study or learn material for work, or if you need to remember specific protocols at work. Gum also injects a little bit of insulin into your blood. This little bit of insulin gives you an added energy boost, reinvigorating your brain and motivating you to get out of that slump that you may find yourself in.

So gum is actually a really effective booster of mental performance. Best of all, unlike many other mental performance enhancers, gum is responsible for all sorts of benefits without any side-effects. The latest investigation into gum comes from a team of psychologists at St. Lawrence University. They conducted an experiment to measure the effect of gum on the brain and whether it actually did help improve performance.

The experiment went like this: 159 students were presented with a number of very demanding cognitive tasks, such as repeating random numbers backward and trying to solve challenging logic puzzles. Half of the subjects chewed gum (sugar-free and sugar-added) while the other half didn't chew anything.

The subjects who were randomly assigned to chew gum significantly outperformed the others in five out of six of the tests. The only exception was in the sixth test, which was in verbal fluency, where subjects needed to name as many words as possible from a given category, such as "animals." The gum's sugar content had no effect on the performance.

Even though it seems hard to believe, gum might just be the answer to your struggling focus. It's a cheap and easy method to try to give you the added push to get you sucked back into your work. If you're not a gum fan, you can still use this research to help you. Gum increases attention span because it increases oxygen flow to the brain. You can replicate this by taking short exercise breaks through your day—even taking just five minutes to tackle some stairs can make you more alert. If you can't exercise, sometimes taking a break to breathe very deeply for a moment or two can be more than helpful.

It improves not only your attention span, but also your memory, which is perfect for helping you get out of any work slumps you may be experiencing. That's not to say that you'll immediately be able to finish that mountain of work you've been avoiding for far too long, but gum may just be a quick way to help get you back on track and focused once more.

What about going beyond chewing and into eating? What kind of effect does that have on your focus and productivity?

Your brain constitutes only 2% of your body weight, and yet it consumes over 20% of your daily energy intake. It's clear that we need to continually refuel to keep ourselves in peak working condition. We might as well follow the circadian rhythm set forth in the previous point. Eating something small roughly every two hours will keep your energy levels replenished and your alertness high. But for every study that tells you what to eat, there is another study that says the opposite (for instance, a study showed that eating protein is more effective because our neurotransmitters are made from amino acids, which can be derived from proteins), so I'll just leave you with the recommendation to eat slightly more frequently than you think you would need to.

Water, on the other hand, there is no debate about. Being dehydrated has been shown to reduce your mental performance a significant percentage. It can also lead to pronounced fatigue and lack of ability to focus. Again, drink more water than you might think necessary and you're on the right track to keeping your body fueled for focus.

It seems that having an oral fixation, whether you intend to swallow it or not, can be hugely beneficial for your productivity.

#13. Implementation Intentions

An *implementation intention* is where you reframe your goals into "if-then" statements. Here, of course, our goal is to be more focused and productive at-will. How can an if-then statement help with that?

Think of matters in the following way: *if* this happens, *then* I will do this. The *if* part is a situation in daily life, and the *then* part is the response of focus. *If* you go to the bathroom, *then* you will reply to three emails afterward. *If* it is 11:00 a.m., *then* you will not reply to emails for two hours. *If* you drive your car, *then* you will listen to educational audiobooks while driving.

It's relatively simple, but more background is always helpful.

The concept of implementation intentions, introduced by Peter Gollwitzer, a professor of psychology at New York University, has been around since 1999. Studies have found this technique causes a whopping 7.7 times greater increase in making progress toward one's goals. The purpose is for you to anticipate a situation and your behavior in response, a response that is aimed toward a specific goal. Take your decision-making power out of the picture; in fact, remove all choice from the matter. The idea is to make it a natural part of the *if* part of the equation so they eventually become associated.

If you are trying to boost your focus, you might want your goal to be reducing phone use. After you set this goal, your thinking should shift to "*if* I am doing work at my desk, *then* I will turn off my phone." This way, you set up a situation and your response to it is one that will help you reach your goal. If you get into a mindset for this example where you can only use your phone when not at your desk, eventually you will reach a point where it's not worth leaving your desk just to use your phone, and instead you will keep working.

Another example might be that you want to exercise more so you can start your day off with some energy. In this case, you might think "*if* I wake up at 7:00 a.m., *then* I will go to the gym." You can try this method with any other scenario as long as it features an if-then statement and is targeted at you reaching a particular goal. You are taking two independent acts and pairing them together in a way that binds them. Instead of instinctively throwing one punch in defense, your instinct becomes to throw two punches in quick succession.

When our minds are given the opportunity to wander and hesitate, they will do so. Implementation intentions remove choices while focusing on situations that you will commonly face, forcing you down a path that you know is the best course of action and one that will ultimately lead to one of your goals.

It automates responses. If you've already decided exactly what you're going to do, then everything becomes significantly easier. This can be applied to everything in life; having a plan even for the smallest things can make everything easier. If you think of the frustration you experience when you're stuck in line behind someone who takes 30 minutes to order a simple coffee, you will understand that decisiveness is the number one ally you can have.

When you've got a plan or decision for something you know will happen, you won't forget to act or miss an opportunity that will benefit you, nor will you waste time deliberating. You will be less swayed in the heat of the moment by those attractive short-term benefits and instead choose the long-term benefits almost automatically.

Finally, this method also conserves willpower. Sticking to a decision drains a lot of willpower, even if we know it is the right thing to do. This method bypasses the fatigue of self-control and decision-making because you already know exactly what you should and will do, and you know that by doing it, you will be one step closer to your goals.

#14. The Power of Nature

The power of nature is a strange one. It has the ability to affect our health and well-being without us even noticing it and can be especially helpful in stressful atmospheres, such as at work. There have been many studies showing not only that our environment can have a positive impact on our moods and attitudes, but that being surrounded by nature can affect our work patterns and habits and allow us to be more productive in our work.

This doesn't mean that if you work in an office (or similar setting) that you need to resign immediately and move to a forest. It doesn't matter where you are, but rather, what you can do to take advantage of the world around you. Research has proven that there are several quick and easy things that you can change in your daily work environment so that you are closer to nature, and thus taking advantage of all the benefits the natural world can provide us.

The Power of Green. Nature can be calming, soothing, inspiring, and grounding, and it turns out that it's also good when you're having trouble focusing on your work. More specifically, staring at an image associated with nature has been found to be a good way to help improve your focus mindset. The *Journal of Environmental Psychology* published a study by the University of Melbourne's Kate Lee and a group of her colleagues about the power of looking at green.

During the experiment, 150 students were asked to press a number on their keyboards which corresponded with the series of numbers that flashed repeatedly on a computer screen, unless the number was three, in which case they were to press nothing at all. The activity was long and tedious and required complete concentration and a high attention to detail for a long time.

At the midway point, half the students took a brief 40-second "microbreak" and looked at a specific image on their screens. The study found that interrupting a tedious, attention-demanding task with a computerized image of a green roof—a roof partially made of vegetation—dramatically improved students' focus and resulted in better overall performance on their task.

After the students were faced with the image of the green roof, they reported that it felt more "restorative" and that they felt as if they performed better on their task. They performed especially well in their response times, lessening their fluctuation in reactions, and made fewer errors of "omission," in this case failing to tap the keyboard key when they saw a number other than three.

Is it because something in us subconsciously recognizes the primal nature of nature? This could just be because sometimes you just need a break from long, monotonous activities in order to reinvigorate yourself. However, it could also be due to the calming effect of nature and its tendency to reduce stress. This is especially true at jobs where you're at a computer all day or reading through paperwork, tasks that can have you feeling physically drained and mentally exhausted.

By breaking up a task that is monotonous and fatiguing and forcing yourself to stare at something that is connected to the natural world, you can actually significantly improve your workflow. A picture or computer background would suffice. Even better, set an alarm and go for a quick walk outside and see nature up close, if you can. This is one of the easiest things to achieve in a busy working environment. Hanging a painting, sticking up a poster, or even just searching the internet will do the trick. After a quick 40-second look, you'll be ready to return to any task.

Natural Light. Harsh lighting and artificial light are everywhere. Long gone are the days where we woke with the sun and slept when it set. In today's modern world, we're always trying to fit in as much work as we can, and we're not always in the best atmosphere to do so. There are several studies that prove working in natural light is extremely beneficial when trying to complete a task, and that too much artificial light can be detrimental in more ways than one.

The Neuroscience Program at Northwestern University conducted one such study. It proved that there is a very strong relationship between workplace daylight exposure and office workers' sleep, activity, and quality of life.

According to the study, employees slept 46 minutes more per night, on average, if they worked in natural light. They also slept more soundly and efficiently and reported a higher quality of life than those who did not work in natural light. Workers who worked in windowless environments had lower scores in their physical health and vitality than those who worked near daylight. They also reported poorer sleep quality, along with sleep disturbances and daytime dysfunction.

Natural light has many health-related benefits and can feel mentally more satisfying as well. A lack of natural light has been documented to disrupt the body's circadian rhythms, which are behavioral changes that respond to light and darkness in one's environment. By disrupting our circadian rhythms, a lack of natural light can cause abnormal sleep patterns and also seasonal affective disorder, which results in symptoms such as depression and lethargy.

All of this means that without natural light, your body will be significantly less productive and energized. If you can, try to change your work environment so that you are exposed to natural light as much as possible. If this is impossible, like if you work in an office that is windowless, you can buy natural light lamps that simulate sunlight.

A study in Britain, published in *The Responsible Workplace*, also supported the importance of natural light. The study showed that of the many factors that influenced the occupants' level of satisfaction with a building, windows were the number one determinant. This is because the value of lighting is significant in two ways. The first is directly, by affecting our vision—what and how well we are able to see. The second is indirectly, by influencing our moods, behavior, and even hormonal balance.

We've all noticed that when the weather is overcast or it's been raining for days, there can be a dreary atmosphere that sticks around until a ray of light breaks through the clouds. This is because of the strong effect of natural light. Natural light renovations have been shown to result in happy workers and a better overall work environment with less absenteeism and fewer illnesses. Furthermore, because of the satisfaction in the workers from the better lighting, the employees also increased their productivity.

In a final study, Christopher Jung of the University of Colorado showed that bright lights can reduce our level of cortisol, which means that we will feel less stressed under bright lighting conditions.

With all of these benefits of natural light, it seems foolish to prevent ourselves from being exposed to it as often as we can. So stop working like a hermit and open your windows to the sun. If you can't do this, find a way to be exposed to natural light, even with a lamp that simulates it if you really have to. Take a walk on your lunch break, sit by a window when you can, or take your work elsewhere. Find a way to bask in the sun's rays, and you'll feel better for it. Just wear sunscreen from time to time.

Plants. The more you learn about plants, the more you realize that they will always have additional benefits. If you are someone who works in a room with plants or vegetation of some sort, even if it's just because you think they're pretty or you needed a simple way to decorate, you're already one step ahead of the game. A workplace surrounded by plants is one where you will be considerably more productive and efficient in your tasks.

Several studies have proven the benefits of working with plants around you, even if it's just that small shrub in the corner. One of these studies demonstrated that employees who were randomly assigned to work in a room filled with plants outperformed those who didn't have access to plants.

Another study, this one conducted in the UK and the Netherlands by Marlon Nieuwenhuis from Cardiff University's School of Psychology, addressed employee perception of plants. When office workers could see a plant from their desks, their perceptions of air quality, concentration, and workplace satisfaction, as well as their objective measures of productivity, all increased.

So why are plants so beneficial to have in a workspace? We are all aware of the oxygen-providing attribute of plants, but they are also able to suck carbon dioxide and other relatively benign toxins from the air. This is why the workers perceived to have cleaner and more concentrated air in their offices. Additionally, plants also appear to provide an overall mental improvement to those in the study. Plants have a considerable calming effect when they surround you, and they've been known to reduce levels of stress. This is perfect for stressful environments like your work. On top of that, plants can help absorb noise, and quiet is often essential for a working environment.

It's not entirely clear just why plants can have such a positive impact on us mentally. Perhaps it's just subconscious or a way to take us out of a stressful work environment by reminding us what's outside or waiting for us when we are finished. Perhaps it's the placebo effect taking hold by the supposed fresher air we are sucking in. Regardless, the evidence is undeniable.

Having a few plants in the office is a quick and easy way to improve your performance and motivation in the office, as well as to visually liven a place up. The benefits of having even a single plant in your workspace are huge. Not only can you make a place more aesthetically pleasing, you can also improve mood, productivity, and overall performance. Just make sure you take care of it, or choose a hardy one if you're not a green thumb, and your plant will do the rest.

Baby Animals. At last, after all those hours spent staring at adorable newborn pandas or sleeping kittens, the research is finally here to back you up. Maybe that urge to look at cute pictures of baby animals isn't as unproductive as you once thought. You can finally let go of the guilt you've been harboring for "wasting time." Research may be able to prove that looking at cute pictures of baby animals can actually help your productivity at work and improve your overall performance and efficiency.

A Japanese research paper has recently been published in the online journal *PloS One* titled "The Power of Kawaii: Viewing Cute Images Promotes a Careful Behavior and Narrows Attentional Focus." It concluded that looking at cute animal images at work could boost your focus, attention to detail, and overall performance on a task.

The study, conducted by Hiroshi Nottono of the University of Hiroshima, studied three different groups of students as they performed several tasks. These tasks ranged from visual tasks to those involving dexterity, with one of the tasks being similar to the American board game Operation. Each group attempted its respective task twice—the first time without looking at any images, and the second time after looking at a series of pictures. These images could have included baby animals, adult animals, or neutral subjects such as foods.

They concluded that the students who viewed cute animal pictures performed far better at their tasks than their peers who viewed pictures of adult animals or food. There are many theoretical explanations linked to this improvement.

One theory involved a behavioral tendency in humans to slow down their speech when talking to babies, puppies, and kittens. Researchers speculated that looking at images of baby animals might have had a similar effect in a slowing down of not just speech, but the behavior of the students. As such, they were more careful and attentive during their tasks, and performed more accurately than their peers.

Another offered explanation was to do with nurturing instincts that may have been brought up when looking at the young animals. The researchers suspected that perhaps those who received an increase in nurturing feelings due to the baby animal pictures might have performed better in care-related tasks that aimed to help someone, even if it was only in the form of a board game.

Whatever the reason, the study determined that the simple act of looking at the photos was enough to increase focus and attention when they were viewed before a task. It stated that, "If viewing cute things makes the viewer more attentive, the performance of a non-motor perceptual task would also be improved."

So if you've been secretly viewing these cute pictures at your desk in the office, trying to hide the fact that you may be doing something unproductive, next time, just go ahead. You could be boosting your productivity without even knowing it.

Generally, the world around us can be far more helpful to our focus and productivity. Nature is all around us, and is one thing that is so easily accessible that it would be a complete waste not to take advantage of everything it can give us. Whether it is surrounding ourselves with greenery, natural light, plants, or cute animals, there is always something the world can give us that may help our concentration and our overall motivation. Nature is another way that our literal environments fuel our focus.

#15. Change Contexts

If you've been sitting in the same cubicle all day, it can be easy for your mind to wander. If I'm reading the same passage over and over, struggling for focus and comprehension, I simply pack up and change my scenery. To me, this is defined as changing everything in my line of sight. This might mean moving to another room, downstairs, upstairs, or to another office or café completely.

It never fails me. I'm instantly starting over with the same amount of focus I had when I arrived there. Changing your scenery will break up the monotony of your day and reinvigorate you. It will also essentially split your days into parts, where one part might be at home, the next part at a café, and the next at the office.

This is significant because for most people, energy is contextual. This means that we have certain amounts of energy for each context. In other words, we have a separate gas tank for each piece of scenery we might find ourselves in. This is because it takes a certain amount of energy to get up, leave, arrive, and then settle in. Then we have natural stages of being alert after movement, exploring our surroundings, and being mentally stimulated by what's new around us.

That's why changing the scenery occasionally is so important. It takes advantage of the fact that you have compartmentalized energy, and you can be completely invigorated by simply altering your physical space.

Just think of changing your scenery as having dinner and the subsequent dessert. Our stomachs have been proven to have separate satiety levels for different types of food. This means that even if you're full from the main course, you'll still be hungry for, and make room for, dessert.

I tend to plan a few tasks for one location, another batch for another location, and still others for my home office. Obviously, you can only move to your next location when you finish your assigned tasks, so it will give you motivation to focus and complete them in record time. You've essentially created an additional incentive.

Beyond the psychological benefits, it breaks up the monotony of your day and wakes you up with physical activity. Changing your scenery can reinvigorate your sense of focus by serving as a creative catalyst. You might be losing focus or becoming distracted because you are staring at the same "I Hate Mondays" cat poster, so seeing and hearing new sounds can help throw your brain into action. You can gain inspiration from hearing a song on the radio outside and galvanize your sense of how to write your report.

You gain a fresh perspective from which to approach your work, and all you needed was a breath of fresh air to manifest a breakthrough.

On a related note, did you know that studying the same material in different locations and environments helps memory retention?

A study by Robert Bjork found that information is remembered and encoded into our memory holistically. This means that if you study Spain in an aquarium, your memory will associate the two subconsciously. Your memory will also associate what you wore that day, what you ate, the smells in the aquarium, and what stood out visually in your environment. They'll all be lumped together, as far as your memory is concerned, with the specific information you are trying to remember or learn. That's a lot of triggers that can help you recall information about Spain.

This means two things. First, that it is possible to evoke the memory of Spain just by being exposed to the same smells and visual stimuli. If they are part of your overall memory of the information, then they will act to remind you of the rest of it. In other words, if you studied Spain in an aquarium and see a picture of an aquarium, it's entirely possible it will remind you of the information you learned about Spain.

Second, if you change locations frequently while learning and processing the same information, you are strengthening your memory because it will be associated with multiple locations, smells, and other stimuli to make you remember it. The researchers deemed this "increased neural scaffolding." The more stimuli that triggers that memory or information, the more deeply it is encoded in your memory like a growing web.

This adds support to the proposition that you should change locations frequently. If you can't change your scenery completely, change what's on your desk, the music you are listening to—anything that impacts any of your five senses. The more change of stimuli, the more roots the information will take to your brain.

#16. Doodle

Yes, doodling—the small scribbles or masterpieces that you create in your notebooks or the tiny stick figures you draw in the margins. Apparently, doodling isn't as undesirable as we were once told in school.

A psychologist from the University of Plymouth, Jackie Andrade, performed a study to test whether doodling really did have an effect on memory and focus. The participants all listened to a monotonous recording and half of them were asked to doodle while the other half were not. When asked to recall the information they'd just listened to, the doodlers demonstrated significantly higher recall that the non-doodlers.

So why is this the case? It may seem that doodling would only serve as a distraction as it might draw your attention onto whatever you're drawing rather than the task you should be focusing on. However, Andrade argues against this. "People may doodle as a strategy to help themselves concentrate ... We might not be aware that we're doing it, but it could be a trick that people develop because it helps them from wandering off into a daydream."

This suggests that instead of distracting you and pulling you away from the task, doodling might just be grounding your thoughts and forcing your mind into a subconscious activity that requires minimal concentration while the rest of you absorbs information.

The scientists hypothesized that unlike daydreaming, which involves a significantly larger mental demand, the mental load required to absentmindedly doodle is quite small and doesn't lead your mind entirely astray from the task that you are supposed to be engaged in. The small iota of your attention that is preoccupied with doodling actually appears to keep you focused and centered in the present time, giving you a release valve from the frustrations of an overly long or tiresome task.

This might also be due to the fact that we are very visual people; our entire world is centered on what you can see. Doing a task such as doodling while you're being bombarded with information can help you form associations, and therefore, you will be able to process things much more efficiently.

American author Sunni Brown is known for advertising the power of doodling. According to her research, doodling can help you "anchor a task." This means that it will keep you focused during a long meeting or phone call. Focus on scribbling pictures or designs that reflect what you're hearing or thinking. It doesn't matter if they are funny or weird, or have nothing to do with what you are discussing. Doodling will help keep your thoughts from straying, and you might be surprised at how much you will be able to recall of a conversation afterward.

If doodling won't work for you, then maybe use the general idea of visual stimuli to help you. When you need to brainstorm ideas, try a pen and paper diagram with as many visual representations as you can. When you have a lot to do, write a physical to-do list and place it somewhere easily accessible so that you will always have it in sight. Or even leave a notebook and pen beside you so that when you hit a stopping point in your work, you can try to reason it out visually. The point is that it may help you organize and focus your thoughts so that you can reach ideas or methods of action.

Takeaways:

- We may be past the difficult first part, as well as the delicate second part, but that doesn't mean we're out of the woods yet. How can we remain focused on a long-term basis? What can we intentionally enact and effectuate, versus just identifying pitfalls to avoid?

- First of all, you should be aware of and take advantage of your circadian rhythm. Studies have shown that during both sleep and waking periods, our bodies run in 90-minute cycles. This means that no matter what, your focus will wane after about 90 minutes. Use this knowledge strategically and be sure to not burn out by pushing too hard. Listen to your body and manage your energy instead of your time.
- Chewing gum has oddly enough been proven to help focus. Staying fueled and hydrated should be less surprising. The brain represents 20% of our body's energy consumption, so it needs to be constantly replenished and hydrated.
- An implementation intention is just an *if-then* statement. For example: *If* it is 10:00 a.m., *then* you will ignore emails for two hours. It takes away your choice and free will. This is actually good, because our present selves often lack the foresight to make optimal decisions.

- Nature is a powerful, curious thing. Natural light, simply seeing green, watching baby animals, and having plants around have all been shown to increase focus and productivity.
- Sometimes what you need to get focused in a change of environment and context. This simply refers to moving locations when your focus and energy are dipping. It helps because there is a certain amount of alertness that a new environment brings because of the new stimuli. Memory has also been shown to improve when learning while being exposed to different settings.
- Finally, doodling has been shown to help focus. This is because doodling essentially acts as an outlet for your frustration, boredom, and desire to procrastinate. Yet it does so in a way that is low-impact and allows you to keep focusing and thinking on a matter at hand.

Section 4. Plan Strategically and Outsmart Yourself

Sometimes, no matter our willpower and how much we have to do, we can't pull it together. We're spent. The brain just does not want to compute anymore for the day.

Does an occasion or two spring to mind for you? If so, it will make you happy to know that these types of situations are almost entirely avoidable. All it takes is some strategic planning before the fact.

Usually when such a solution is promised, it ends up being a lot more work than is worthwhile. Here, planning to maximize your focus is largely about understanding yourself a little bit better and prioritizing what really matters to you. This way, you can outsmart and outwit your lazy tendencies before they get the chance to surface.

This is the section where you are truly learning to put yourself in the best position for success. There are numerous methods to help plan for productivity, and while they might not all work for you, you're certain to find a couple that do.

#17. Diagnose Your Focus

Cut your losses. The first time I heard that phrase was when I was dating my first girlfriend. I didn't quite know what my friends meant by it, but I didn't think it was positive. It turned out they weren't fans of hers and were telling me to cut my losses by not investing any more time or energy into a relationship they saw as doomed.

Cutting your losses means accepting a defeat or cost of some sort, and making your peace with it before the defeat or cost grows even larger. Accept the current loss and leave the situation without trying to mitigate it or gain back what you've put into it. It's another way of saying that to win the war, you must sometimes lose battles. In taking a step back, you'll eventually set yourself up to take two steps forward.

It's the same with productivity. Sometimes you just have to know when to cut your losses and stop working, regardless of how little you've gotten done. Rarely will the extra few hours you spend "grinding" at the office be worth it if you're not in the correct frame of mind. More likely than not, you'll just be creating a negative association with working hard and make yourself work-averse in the future.

It's completely normal to lose steam, or to not be in the mood for work from time to time. There's only so much work you can do in a day. Some days you just don't have it. So why push? There's a reason famous author Stephen King famously limits his writing time to 20 hours a week—he knows he will start to lose focus and the quality of his writing will suffer if he works beyond those 20 hours. He has still published over 50 novels in his career; perhaps it's because he sets limits like this, not in spite of it, that he has been able to be so prolific.

In the best of times, our brains are sponges. But sometimes they get so filled they turn into boulders that are useless to their purpose. This is when it's quitting time.

Diagnose your focus and learn to recognize when you should take a break. Stop working at 50% capacity and come back when you can go forward at full steam.

By learning how to identify when you're losing focus, you can take countermeasures that will boost your overall productivity, or smartly cut your losses for the day. The key to solving a problem is to first correctly identify it. In essence, you are paying attention to your attention, which is notoriously difficult unless you have some objective milestones to look for.

Different people get mentally fatigued in different ways. When you're mentally tired, you stop focusing, you stop solving problems, and you stop creating. Instead, you're essentially burning time and switching between tasks, trying to find the easiest one to dive into. That's the first sign you should cut your losses—when you keep refreshing your email to try to find something small to do. You keep switching between tasks in the hopes of finding something easy. It's productive procrastination at its finest. You feel like you might be accomplishing something, but in reality, you're doing nothing.

If you find that you're beating around the bush, it's your brain's way of telling you it wants a break. This should be differentiated from simple procrastination, where you appear to have energy to do *other* things. Here, nothing seems appealing or possible.

The second sign is when you physically avoid your work instruments, like your computer or notepad. You know you have lost focus when you are rearranging your desk or emptying your pencil sharpener. You stand up and walk around. You avoid looking at the computer or touching your tablet. At that point, anything else becomes more attractive than actual work.

The third sign you are losing focus is when you physically get tired or sleepy. Your work is not making it into your brain anymore, and anything you produce while in this state will essentially be gibberish. It's like when you fall asleep during a lecture and wake to find your notes have trailed off into unintelligible scribbles, then stopped altogether. You probably would have been better off going home, taking a nap, and reviewing someone else's notes afterwards.

The fourth sign is when you read or do something once, then immediately read or do it again because it didn't register with you. This is the height of distraction, because you can't even focus on a passage of 100 words without your mind wandering off somewhere else.

Learn how to recognize these signals. You can't solve a problem if you can't identify it. Everyone is different, and you'll have to examine your habits and behaviors.

This point is just a complicated way of saying that you shouldn't always try to push through tasks. When you do this, you are basically throwing gasoline on a raging fire of unproductivity. It's not going to solve anything. You've already lost focus, and trying to waste your willpower in that state of mind is a bad use of resources.

Don't work through it. You can't use brute force to get through everything. This is the same reason all-nighters are rarely as productive or helpful as you think.

It is uniquely difficult to diagnose your focus because you are trying to gain self-awareness about when you are unaware. Sometimes, you'll have to cut your losses in favor of better overall focus.

#18. Create Daily Goals

If you've ever gone grocery shopping out of boredom instead of necessity, you probably filled up your shopping cart with impulse purchases and justified them with, "Why not?"

How did you end up with marshmallows in December and nothing that could comprise a full meal? It's not like you're going to have a bonfire anytime soon, but hey—*why not*? You've never cooked with mushrooms before, and rarely cook anything but overdone pasta, but you thought you might try to make a mushroom soufflé this weekend because—*why not*?

When you attempt to accomplish a goal (satisfying hunger) without a game plan (a shopping list), the results are often less than optimal. You get distracted and lose sight of what you really want to do. On the contrary, if you were to head to the grocery store with a list of five items for a specific recipe, you would probably just grab those items and be on your way.

When you create a habit out of listing your goals, you create focus and don't allow yourself to deviate as much as you would without a list. It prevents your mind from wandering because it is set on a defined path with no room for thought or second-guessing.

In the grocery store without a list, you wander up and down every aisle and are distracted by whatever catches your eye, usually foods you shouldn't be eating. In productivity without a list, you also wander around each different task and get distracted by whatever catches your eye. And then, when checkout time comes for both, you end up paying much more (in money and time) than you should!

To maximize your productivity and output, you can't allow yourself to wander around your desk or office aimlessly. You need to make sure you can stay focused on a daily basis. Just like in the grocery store, you can't depend on your willpower in the moment—temptations and distractions are emotional by nature. Therefore, make your decisions ahead of time while you are ruled by discipline and have a clear view of your future goals.

This all culminates in creating a *daily goals checklist*. You can call this a to-do list, but I prefer the term "daily goals" because it emphasizes the need to constantly re-evaluate your priorities.

You might not be able to achieve all your goals that day, but you stand a pretty high chance because of the focus the list creates. Instead of freestyling, you'll face constant reminders of what your priorities are along with a semblance of structure.

Daily goals checklists keep you working toward your bigger goals while allowing you to tune everything else out, the latter of which is equally important. What's the optimal way to create your daily goals checklist?

First, write your daily goals checklist the night before.

Start your day prepared to hit the ground running. Don't make the mistake of working out your daily goals checklist in the morning.

Mornings are notoriously hazy and disorienting, and before you realize it, you'll have spent an hour on your daily goals checklist while at the same time reading your emails. You'll also probably have a skewed sense of priorities, because you'll fixate on tasks that are easier instead of those that are most important.

When you write your list the night before, you'll have a clear and objective view of what you need to accomplish the next day, and you won't be influenced by the morning's inclination toward laziness and procrastination. You'll have the clarity of mind to properly think through what's truly important to do, and you will therefore prioritize your tasks accordingly.

Second, create a mixture of small, easy tasks, and large, tedious, or difficult tasks.

We all have a finite amount of willpower and energy with which we start our days. This means we have to ration wisely to make sure we don't constantly feel as if we're slaying dragons. It's incredibly discouraging to finish a large task only to be instantly faced with an even larger, more daunting one. You'll avoid the task and procrastinate, so sandwich your small tasks with large tasks. You can also substitute tasks you enjoy with those you detest— whatever method allows you to allocate your willpower effectively.

Those easy and enjoyable tasks also make good sense to start your day with because they will break the inertia in your brain and create momentum. If it helps, you can group items by amount of time they should take so you can sort them accordingly. You can also group items by perceived difficulty and mental load.

It's tough to get started working when you're facing a few tasks that will each take hours to complete. Take the opportunity the night before to plan an easier life for yourself. Start the day with something that is easy, or that you might even be excited about it. Build momentum and warm your brain up with easier tasks.

It can even be a task that you've left partially unfinished from the day before, one that you can easily complete in the morning to get into the swing of productivity. This may not make sense initially, but it gives you an easy win and reason to sit down.

Third, daily goals checklists must be realistic, but they should also be aspirational and slightly out of reach.

Filling your list with *slightly* more than you normally would accomplish in a day can be extremely motivating and decrease the amount of procrastination you indulge in. It will push you every day and keep you racing to maximize your output.

Psychological studies show that the most effective goals are only slightly above your level because you can easily imagine their completion: you just need to increase your rate of speed. You'll create a bit of pressure for yourself and enjoy a sense of achievement after you accomplish more than you thought you would or could.

Finally, get everything onto a single page so you can then take a broader look at your priorities. The power of the list is its ability to organize your focus. Make your list every night before you sleep and you'll wake up knowing exactly what to do.

#19. Categorize Tasks

A straightforward to-do list can be just as unproductive as having nothing at all. It can make you spin your wheels, create anxiety, and cause more confusion than it should. Everyone operates differently, and categorizing tasks presents a solution slightly different from a daily goals checklist.

After finishing a task, you can very easily slip into the danger pit that arises when you attempt to select your next task, creating a loss of focus. Just think about the uptick in efficiency you would create if you had to make one hundred phone calls and you kept the phone to your ear between calls. Once you put the phone down, you'll inevitably find a reason to wander off before the next call.

This occurs if you only list every task you need to complete without priority or organization. If you've got a to-do list that simply lists 10 tasks, how do you even know where to start? Do you start from the top and work your way down to the bottom? What if you start in the middle? What if you get stuck on the first task?

You can spend 10 minutes trying to make sense of your task landscape every time you glance at it, or you can use categories to effectively milk the most from your list.

A list for a list's sake doesn't accomplish everything you need it to in an efficient way, it only ensures you don't forget tasks completely. Of course, this is valuable in itself to reducing your stress and anxiety, but we are striving for more than that. Break your to-do list into categories that will let you know exactly how to spend each minute of your day.

Here are the five categories I suggest for your upgraded to-do list. They are ordered from top to bottom in terms of priority—because that's what matters. This is how you squeeze productivity out of every waking minute. The categories work sequentially; only when you feel that you're done with the prior category should you move onto the next.

Category One: Immediate Attention

Immediate attention—well, that's self-explanatory, isn't it? Check this one first and stay here until it is empty. These are the tasks that you must do that day, or even every hour. There might be deadlines associated with them, either internal or external.

Order tasks within this category from most urgent to least. This is the first category to address when you look at your to-do list. Everything else for the day is just a bonus and nice to have. In fact, you should block everything else out until these items are completed because nothing else matters. Don't look at the other categories until your *Immediate Attention* items are done.

Within this category, you should order the tasks from most urgent to least. This is where the essential work is and where you should focus your efforts.

For a teacher, *Immediate Action* items might be grading homework assignments or writing a test to be given the very next day. Things for the following week can be ignored and put off until later.

Category Two: In Progress

These are tasks you have been working on or that might be longer-term in nature.

They are not urgent. *In Progress* items are for all intents and purposes what you were planning to begin your day with, except for the fire drill of the *Immediate Attention* tasks.

You may not be able to finish them that day or hour, but you should check in to see how they are progressing *after* you've attended to your most urgent *Immediate Attention* items. These are also items that might need incremental work every day, so make sure to meet your daily responsibility to them.

These tasks won't make it into the *Immediate Attention* category because they can't be accomplished in one day or sitting, so their urgency is lower. Still, this should be the second category you check to make sure that long-term or frequent projects are indeed moving along as they should. Often, these appear to be more important than they are because they are always present. But don't let that fool you—there will likely be no quick consequences for missing these items.

For a teacher, *In Progress* items might be monitoring grades, dealing with emails from parents, or organizing a field trip for next week. These are all things that need to occur on a regular basis, but they can always slide down in priority when urgent matters come.

Category Three: Follow-ups

These are items that aren't necessarily in your control, but you need to check up on them to make sure they are moving along. This category is outward-facing and focused on corresponding with others and checking on tasks in motion. Most of the time, your emails and calls can be pushed down to this level of priority. This is an especially frustrating category because it feels like you should be doing something about them, even though there is nothing to do. The items in this category feel mentally unfinished, and they unfortunately occupy a space in your brain.

Things you might list here are to remind others about something, to follow up on a project, or to call someone back. This is also where you take note of tasks about which you have not heard back. In a sense, this is similar to the "don't do" list—they are not your responsibility, and you don't have to actively do anything besides check-in with people.

This category is mainly for checking the progress of tasks that have made it out of the prior two categories. If they have been stalled on something unrelated to you, your job still isn't done yet!

Even so, these don't warrant a higher priority because the main focus isn't on you. You just want to make sure they will be ready for you when you need them.

For a teacher, *Follow-up* items might be making sure all permission slips have been signed, and organizing a teacher's luncheon is on track. None of these rests on the teacher himself at the moment, but they *involve* him overall.

Category Four: Upcoming

The *Upcoming* tasks are a category you want to keep your peripheral vision on.

These are things that might be tomorrow or next week, or they might depend on the current tasks you are finishing up now.

Whatever the case, they aren't things you should currently devote your time to. They are the next dominos to fall, and what you should proactively plan for so you have a clear idea of what the rest of your week or month looks like. This category is about setting yourself up for the future, versus doing something for the present moment.

It's a good idea to plan out your *Upcoming* tasks as far ahead of time as possible, and simply be aware of what's going to be on your docket on any given day or week.

This ensures you don't miss anything by constantly thinking about what your next steps are. What will you need to focus on once your current docket is clear, and what kind of urgency will those items require once they become current?

This is the category of tasks that people can most stand to improve on. We all know what tasks are urgent and require our primary and secondary efforts, but what about what follows? Focusing more attention to this category will help you maintain better focus in the long run.

For a teacher, *Upcoming* items might be thinking ahead to group projects for the next unit, and projecting when you will run out of construction paper. These won't come into play for days, if not weeks, but understanding what's to come is important in pacing and focus.

Category Five: Ideas

This category should resemble more of a list of ideas and tasks that you want to explore. They are aspirational. It might say something like "Phone as a memory recorder?" These are ideas that you can't devote time to immediately and are therefore your last priority, but you still need to keep them in mind.

Take notes on your future projects whenever you can and they will take shape sooner rather than later. These ideas will often start as big picture tasks, and then break down into small, manageable chunks and tasks. You might spend a lot more time here than you think because nothing else can actively be worked on at the moment. Remember, that doesn't mean nothing is happening; it's just that your role is paused for the time being.

This category is about planning for the future and long-term success. If you have extra time, this is something you can work on developing, but not until the rest of the categories are accounted for—those are higher priorities to take care of and manage. *Ideas* is the last category you check. It's a luxury to be able to reach this category. It allows a level of thoughtfulness and attention that we tend to ignore.

For a teacher, *Ideas* items might be researching next year's curriculum and new ideas for class field trips. Getting into the habit of brainstorming new ideas and areas for improvement is certainly going to set this teacher up for success.

Remember, the objective of categorizing your to-do list is to cut down on the mental effort involved in thinking, "What should I be doing right now?" It gives you a clear blueprint as to where your efforts are needed.

If it takes you five to 10 minutes every time you look at your list to figure out where you should be, that's a massive inefficiency that needs to change. If you institute categories, you'll know exactly what you should be doing at any minute of the day with just a quick glance.

#20. ABCDE Your Priorities

And yet to-do lists aren't the best solution for some people. Everyone processes tasks and priorities in different ways, so this shouldn't be a surprise.

Luckily, I've experimented extensively with how to tackle your day. Categories, priorities, models—sometimes it just takes a different approach to resonate with different people. It's called the *ABCDE Priority List.*

This method involves filtering your list based on the amount of negative consequences you will face. That's just how some of us prefer to operate—by knowing what's at stake and working to avoid that pain. This allows you to catalog your time, focus on immediate priorities, and making sure nothing slips through the cracks.

Just as importantly, it will also let you know what you *don't* need to worry about, so you can decrease your mental strain and focus on one thing at a time.

The ABCDE Priority List has five categories.

"A" = Very Important

An "A" task means the item is very important and needs to be done immediately. It is your first priority. You can't wait on others for this, and you're the only one that action depends on.

You *must* take care of it today, and there are serious negative consequences if you fail to do so. It's a strict deadline that overrides any of the other tactics in this book—you simply need to get this done first or second.

Regardless of the stakes, there will be harm if you don't complete this "A" task. That's the easiest way to tell whether an item is truly very important, or if it's a lower priority item. If your life will be negatively affected from failure to complete something that day, it belongs in the "A" category. This includes your own internal deadlines.

Urgency level: that hour or day.

Teacher example: writing a test that you will give later that day.

"B" = Important

In the "B" section of your priority list, you should include items that you *should* do that day.

Compare these with "A" items. "A" items are the things you *must* do. If you don't do those, there will be significant negative consequences.

"B" tasks don't create consequences of that magnitude, which is how you differentiate "A" from "B" tasks. The consequences of not completing an "A" task might be catastrophic and unredeemable, whereas the consequences of not completing a "B" task might be fixable and minor in the long run.

It may be worth skipping over a "B" task solely to complete an "A" task. This fallout will be worth it for the greater good of the "A" task.

Incidentally, this is what separates "B" items from the rest of the hierarchy. There are still negative consequences with the failure to complete a "B" task, but there are none for "C," "D," and "E" tasks.

Following up with others and making sure things are on track to be completed or replied to are also "B" tasks.

Urgency level: after "A" tasks, whether at the end of the day or the next day.

Teacher example: give homework for that night and prepare a lecture for the next day.

"C" = Nice to Do

In any priority list, there are always optional items you keep around just to make sure you don't forget about them. Many people tend to confuse these items with the necessary tasks for the day, which makes this category all the more important.

As the category title says, these are tasks that would be *nice to do*. They aren't necessary for the day, and there is nothing riding on their completion. They're extra, and exist purely if you want to work ahead or start a new initiative.

They might bring secondary value to the other tasks you have, and they might position you for better opportunities in the future. "C" tasks aren't about the present, they are about thinking ahead and working for the future.

Having a good handle on "C" tasks is what will truly double your output. We all know our "A" and "B" tasks, but we rarely catalog what we should do with our extra time (besides relax). We don't think about how we can systematically get ahead and set ourselves up for the future.

For example, networking, sending cold emails, meeting with new potential business partners, and updating your resume are all "C" tasks. So are tasks that you've put off for longer periods of time, like chores and taxes. They are future-facing.

There aren't any negative consequences if you don't do these things, just lost opportunities.

Urgency level: at the end of the day or whenever there is time during the week.

Teacher example: work on your curriculum for the next semester.

"D" = Delegate

These are the tasks you can delegate to coworkers, friends, or outsource completely. They are tasks you shouldn't be doing, and can put onto other people with no negative repercussions.

Keep in mind that there is a big difference between delegation and outsourcing. Delegation means there are people working under you. Outsourcing, on the other hand, involves other people doing *your* job.

"D" tasks are simply things others can do to lessen your workload. Often, they are tasks that *should* be taken care of by others and that you should let go of and trust someone else to do. "D" tasks are often a waste of time to do yourself. They can probably be done by somebody else at the same level of quality.

When you're faced with a "D" task, you must ask yourself whose responsibility it should be, and if the answer is you, who you can ask to help share the burden. This priority level is an act of taking things off your plate, which is a precursor to the next priority level.

Teacher example: you can outsource or delegate decorating the classroom to the students themselves. You could do this, but it doesn't necessarily have to be your responsibility. You can make it an opportunity for the students to be creative and create art.

"E" = Eliminate

These are tasks that you should forget completely. This concept is similar to the "don't-do" list.

You can eliminate more tasks than you think with zero negative consequences. In many cases, these tasks just weigh on your mind and may overwhelm you with a false sense of urgency and emotional stress.

Additionally, when they occupy space on your to-do list, you are unable to escape the mental strain associated with thinking about them.

What should you eliminate? Tasks that suffer from diminishing returns, that are already delegated, that are waiting for input from others, and that simply aren't necessary to your goals within the next month or two. File future aspirations away in a separate folder and keep them out of your daily field of vision. These are typically things that other people will ask of you for their own purposes.

Teacher example: detailed reports on each child's grasp of physical education.

The ABCDE Priority List is a method of making your life more streamlined and focused.

#21. Live In Your Calendar

I've extolled the virtues of to-do lists (with modifications) throughout this section, but it should be noted that there are numerous alternatives to these lists to increase your productivity.

The most effective tactic is the one you will use consistently, and it's been my aim to introduce you to a number of them so you can experiment and choose for yourself.

One of the prevailing opinions in productivity theories comes from the to-do list camp. The thinking is that once you have everything laid out in front of you, you can organize your priorities from there and make sure no stone is left unturned. The allure of the to-do list is to ensure that you are aware of the tasks, A to Z, for which you are responsible.

The other prevailing belief about productivity is to live in your calendar. Instead of inputting your tasks into a list that is static and lacking context, put them in your calendar.

When you put tasks in your calendar, you can plan them in concurrence with the realities of your day. This means you can also plan them based on how long they'll take and where you'll be physically—things any type of task list will lack.

In this way, you can account for literally every minute of your waking day in an extremely accurate manner because you aren't planning in a vacuum. A task list won't account for a dentist appointment, your aversion to working from home, or being tired after your daily gym session. Living in your calendar can account for all of those and create proper expectations for your focus and productivity.

So, how do you live in your calendar?

First, you'll have to know what you need to accomplish on a weekly basis. Lay a calendar or planner in front of you and assign a time slot for each task on each day.

There are 168 hours in any given week, and once you fill in your calendar, you'll know exactly what you should be doing at each moment.

This is a relatively straightforward method. You can visually represent how long and complex each task is and get a far better sense for what you will be able to accomplish during the day and week. You'll know how to manage your time better, what's realistic, and how not to overcommit to people and work.

Arrange your calendar carefully every day and you won't have to debate what to do next. It's in your schedule. There's no decision to be made—it's in your schedule. Wondering what to prepare yourself for? Never fear—it's in your schedule.

But there is an extra layer of thought involved because you have to account for where you'll be and what resources will be available to you. What else should you take into consideration as your complete the puzzle of your week?

- Your energy levels and circadian rhythm.
- How long each task will realistically take, and how much time you should allot to it.
- How focused you feel in relationship to food and exercise.
- The locations you'll be in and how conducive they are to focus.
- Breaks.
- Other commitments.
- Your work habits and how long it takes you to get focused after breaks or finishing a task.
- Free hours for urgent matters that might pop up.
- The people around you and how that contributes to or damages your focus.
- How much you can actually do in a day or week—just because you have a free time slot doesn't mean you can be productive in it!

Having a calendar instantly puts you into the context of your day. That's the biggest weakness and downfall of the to-do list—

the inability to forecast the setting of each task and take daily life into consideration.

With a simple to-do list, all of your tasks, regardless of priority or urgency, look the same on a piece of paper. Nothing about the availability of time along with the non-work related tasks and appointments in our lives is addressed. Without this information, you may not be able to intelligently decide how to spend your time.

Deciding what task to handle at what time injects context as a factor and makes your choices far more justifiable and logical, and thus easy to follow through with. It completely eliminates decision fatigue in the middle of the day and allows you to focus on one task, and then the next task at the top of the hour.

Of course, following the fashion of previous points in this section, make sure to schedule your high priority items first, and then let the lower priority tasks fill in the spaces where they can. This is an instance of where your to-do list categories, or your ABCDE identifications, can integrate well with living in your calendar. It's just logical—if you had an important appointment with your doctor, you would block off the time for that and force everything else to accommodate it.

As a final best practice for living in your calendar, schedule your tasks for a slightly shorter period than you think they might take. If you think a task might take two hours, consider allotting yourself only an hour and 45 minutes or an hour and a half to get it done. Impose a deadline for yourself and create pressure to not fall behind in the calendar of your day.

It just might force you to work a bit quicker and more efficiently, and tune out your distractions in pursuit of staying on track in your calendar. After all, we tend to work a little quicker when our backs are against the wall, don't we?

#22. Default Decisions

Finally, in planning to be focused, we should turn to our environments to help us out. Even though we know what we want to do, most of us have the freedom to make a wide range of choices at any given moment. This can wreak havoc with achieving focus because researchers have found that we often make decisions based on our immediate environment.

This is one of the most predictable of all human traits—tendency to be lazy and reach for the lowest hanging fruit. Whatever is even 1% easier is what we'll do the majority of the time because our willpower is not unlimited.

Our *default decision* is usually whatever happens to be the easiest option, so make them support your goal of being focused and productive. Make being focused 1% easier in your environment, and you'll choose it more.

If you keep your smartphone next to your bed, checking email or social media as soon as you wake up is likely to be your default decision. Instead, what if you kept your phone in a separate room? Keeping alcohol in the house is likely to make drinking consistently a default decision. Instead, what if you only bought water?

Therefore, it makes sense to arrange our environments to create the results we want.

Using the example of losing five pounds, how can we set up our immediate environment in a way that supports our goal? We can stock the kitchen with a variety of portion-controlled healthy snacks so we're ready when a snack attack strikes. We can spend a weekend afternoon preparing nourishing meals for the week ahead so we don't end up making a last-minute fast food run because there's "nothing good" in the house. Placing the dog's leash in plain sight serves as a reminder for us to get out and get moving instead of plopping down on the couch with a bowl of buttery popcorn. Placing a set of hand weights next to the TV reminds us that we can multitask by doing bicep curls while watching our favorite show.

The same kind of environmental changes can be made for focusing. Make distractions more difficult, and make focus easier. Have a designated area for your distractions, such as your phone, and make them difficult to reach. Make it impossible to stand up without encountering a task you've been putting off.

Each one of these small, simple tweaks to our usual routine makes a positive impact and moves us in the direction of success.

Whatever your goals are, there are at least five ways you can tailor your environment to assist with them, whether it be through reminders (posters, alarms), making actions more difficult or easy (only healthy food, a "no elevators" rule), or switching environments altogether (going to the office, getting a desk too small to hold snacks).

Takeaways:

- Sometimes we just don't have the willpower to focus as we like. This may often be the case, actually. Thankfully, we have the opportunity to plan against our worst tendencies and guarantee that we are doing what we need to do in a timely manner.

- The first way to plan strategically for focus is by diagnosing your focus. This is paying attention to how well you can pay attention. At some point, you will just need to take a loss for the day and stop completely. This break prevents burnout, and is actually much more preferable to grinding it out and trying to forge ahead at 50% mental capacity. You just won't get much done, you'll create a negative association with hard work, and you'll waste your time. Know when to cut your losses!

- A daily goals checklist you can think of as a to-do list. Create this the night before so you can think clearly and objectively, instead of emotionally and in reaction to your day. This list decreases your stress because you've got everything laid out and nothing will fall through the cracks. For each day, create a mixture of easy and difficult tasks so you can program in mental breaks. Finally, be a little bit aspirational in your daily workload.

- Instead of a to-do list, you can categorize your tasks. This is helpful because it provides greater context to what you should be focusing on. There are five categories: Immediate Attention, In Progress, Follow-up, Upcoming, and Ideas. Don't move to the next category until you finish everything in the current one.
- Similarly, you can organize your tasks by using ABCDE priorities. The priority levels are determined on the consequences you will receive. "A" and "B" levels have negative consequences and "C" is a bonus, while "D" and "E" have positive benefits.
- For a more three-dimensional and thorough look at your tasks, try scheduling them all in your calendar. This takes significant work beforehand, but it takes your life, habits, tendencies, and energy levels into account. You do not live in a vacuum, and your calendar can reflect this.
- Finally, you can arrange your environment to assist your ability to focus by manipulating your default

decisions. Default decisions are what humans will do most of the time just because they are easiest and cost us the least effort. You can make your distractions cost you more effort, and make focus as easy as sitting down.

Section 5. Making Time Your Friend

Time. Is it your best friend, or your worst enemy?

When you're doing something you love, it's your worst enemy because it always seems to run out too soon, and you never seem to have enough. When you're doing something you hate, it's your best friend because it's the only thing keeping you from freedom and pleasure. Or is it the other way around?

No matter the case, time is what you're going to have to deal with if you want to improve your focus. Whether you have too much of it, too little, or just the right amount, you'll need to start thinking about it in ways you never have before.

Time will always keep on running, but how can we change our perspective to be more focused, productive, and relentless?

#23. Protect Your Time

People are inherently selfish. They'll ask things of you and not offer to reciprocate, often thinking nothing of it. Of course, most people are relatively subtle about this, or we would disown most of our friends. You might even do it yourself.

The biggest way people subtly, and sometimes unknowingly, act selfishly is when they monopolize your time. When given the opportunity, many of your friends or coworkers will hog your time and leave little for your own tasks and interests.

It could be as simple as guilt-tripping you to come to an event, trapping you in conversations that are entirely about them, or inviting you for coffee to "*pick your brain*." These are all selfish motivations that you've likely wanted to avoid and find a way out of before.

To punch out procrastination and extend your focus, you need to take your time back from other people. You'll need to start protecting it as a means to protecting your focus.

It's tough to say no to your friends, but if you spend all of your time doing things you feel obligated to do, people simply won't respect your time. They may still respect you, but they'll know they can have you there at a moment's notice, and they will take you for granted.

Luckily, you can do this in a very diplomatic way. To make people respect your time and earn more freedom for yourself, *make others act first.*

Instead of flat-out refusing their request for your time, or telling them to leave your vicinity (two awkward options at best), create a *small hoop* that people have to jump through before you actually give them your time. You are acting as your own gatekeeper in a sense.

The best way I've managed to put this into practice is with a pre-meeting email or act. If someone wants an uninterrupted block of my time, and I think it might be detrimental to my focus or productivity, I ask them to follow up with me via email about their concern or question *before* I actually meet with them, and I'll get back to them when I can.

This accomplishes two things: It allows me to continue uninterrupted, and it puts the burden of action on someone else and allows me to sit back and wait. This also applies when people ask me to attend events I'm not so keen on, so you can use it in both your personal and professional life.

I've found this simple condition weeds out the majority of requests for my time simply because most people can't be bothered to send me the requested email about their question. Well, if they can't be bothered to spend five minutes doing something for me, why would I spend an hour with them?

If they aren't willing to do that, then it clearly wasn't a burning question that would have led to a productive conversation. It would have been entirely for their benefit, or just a complete waste of my time.

Since this actually weeds out the majority of people who want to utilize my time, it's my diplomatic way of saying no. Even with most of the people who do actually send the pre-meeting email, I can answer their questions with a few written sentences and it saves both of our time... especially mine, because it forced them to accurately define their questions.

Out of 10 potential coffee meetings, three might actually follow up via email, and I'll be able to quickly and efficiently answer two out of those three questions via email. This turns 10 meetings into one, which is a great win for your productivity and getting people to respect your time. I've also pinpointed the people I can really help in an in-depth way.

Now, it's not that I mind meeting with people who want help. I've had a lot of help along the way, and many of those same coffee meetings have been invaluable to my personal and professional growth. I love helping people whenever I can, but I simply can't afford to indulge everyone who wants to chat at the expense of my own daily output. And neither can you: you have your daily priorities, so don't become a part of someone else's to-do list.

This is a book about maximizing your focus, and these are the steps you must implement in your life to make the most of your every waking hour!

Applying a specific process to gaining actual face-time with you will make people aware that you are indeed busy. There are certainly times for meeting new people, but it's not when you're trying to maximize your productivity.

All you're doing is making people aware of the schedule you're working in. They can work their way into it, and if they want to just hang out and indulge themselves, they have to do so outside of that schedule.

If people want something from you, they should be willing to work for it. It's more than common courtesy; it's common sense. If you do someone a favor, they should put in as much of the legwork as possible and make it easy for you to complete.

What about when people just show up in your office, at your door, in your cubicle, or at your lunch table unannounced? How can you protect your time then?

That's when we need to talk about how direct you want to be. If you don't mind being direct, then you don't really need to seek advice here. You already know what to do. But if you're like 99% of the population, the very idea of being so direct in a negative manner makes you anxious.

Let's say that you're working hard at your desk and your resident chatterbox sits down next to you. What's your first move?

"Hey, nice to see you. Just to let you know I'm working on this and need to concentrate soon, so I can only spare a couple of minutes right now... until about 10:40." In this scenario, it's 10:36.

For the serial violator, this simple statement at the outset is to set the tone and set up your escape route at the beginning instead of the end—because we all know it can be tough to squeeze those words out at the end of a conversation. If you just preempt the problem, you give yourself a clear exit.

If your violator doesn't instantly leave and catch you later, then you have free reign to look at your watch or phone and mention the time in a surprised and shocked manner. For instance, "Oh, wow, it's already 10:42! Okay, I need to get back to this, can I catch up with you later?"

Make a show of looking at the time and emphasizing its importance. This should in theory cue your violator to leave. Make sure to add the touch of asking people for permission to find them later—no one will ever say no to that request, and it lets you come off as generous. You can even add an addendum of not wanting to be rude and apologizing for being so busy and such.

People don't understand subtle hints—or at least, the people that you want to leave never will—so protecting your time is a matter of saying exactly what you mean without an impolite impact. It's easy to miss the mark because you're essentially saying, "I don't want to see you right now," but that's not personal and doesn't mean you *never* want to see them. It's about conveying that you've just reached your limits and need to prioritize yourself for the time being.

Protect your time, because time is opportunity, money, pleasure, and everything good in your life. In fact, what's the most valuable possession you own? It's not anything material—it's your time.

Time is the one asset that you will never be able to get back, make up for, or replace.

Once the minute you spend reading this sentence passes, you'll never get it back (but of course, reading this sentence is a minute well-spent).

Time gives you *opportunity*.

Each new minute you're alive, you have the opportunity to do something. You can choose from an infinite number of choices. You can plan ahead, work on something, communicate with people, entertain yourself, or eat. There are so many possibilities when you have time at your disposal.

Once that block of time is gone, it's gone forever. You can't hop on a time machine and get it back. It is finite. You only get one bite of the apple. The sun won't always rise the next day, and you don't want to be asking yourself what you could have done differently each day.

Protect your time and cherish it. Make sure you're doing exactly what you want, within reason. A significant part of this is not squandering your time with choices that appear to be necessary, but actually suck up your happiness and opportunities.

Don't do things out of obligation. When you feel obligated to do something, that means you don't see your own happiness or benefit in it. It is solely for someone else's benefit, and it provides little or no value for you. You're probably just acting to avoid guilt or other negative feelings.

Some might say it is selfless and giving, but remember your own time is worth more than gold! If you're putting other people at a higher priority than you are yourself, it will just lead to unhappiness and a sense of waste.

If you feel there are other more important and pressing things you should be doing, do those instead. If you simply don't want to do something, don't do it. If you know you're not going to be happy doing something or going somewhere, evaluate where your priorities should lie.

Don't spend time with negative people. Negative people suck out your energy. They are motivation vampires. In many cases, misery loves company. They are negative, and they just want other people to be negative as well. They look at life as a horrible ordeal they need to get through, and nothing makes them happier than turning otherwise positive people into people like them.

It's damaging to your productivity and damaging to your quality of life.

Likewise, if you don't feel excited to see someone, it's a strong sign you could be using your time in a way that makes you happier, and thus more productive. Much of the time, we never realize that someone is a drag on us until we take a step back and really think. They may be important people in our lives, but if they make you annoyed, frustrated, or unhappy after seeing them, then what is the point of the relationship?

Maximize your leisure time. Taking advantage of your time isn't all about maximizing your productivity or avoiding activities that don't add value to your life.

It's also about maximizing your leisure time, and making sure you enjoy the free time you do have in the way you want to enjoy it. This means that instead of squandering an afternoon watching golf and snoozing on your couch, you should take note of your favorite activities and hobbies and proactively schedule them for your free time!

Valuing your time is the ultimate precursor to productivity.

#24. Parkinson Knows

British historian Cyril Parkinson was a man of many talents, but for the purposes of this section, we'll focus on the two laws that were eventually named after him, both of which can be related to focus and productivity.

The first of these laws is called *Parkinson's Law of Triviality,* also known as the bike shed effect.

The story behind the law is that there was a committee tasked with designing a nuclear power plant. This was obviously a large undertaking, so appropriate care had to be taken in addressing the safety mechanisms and environmental implications of building a new nuclear power plant.

The committee met regularly and was able to quell most safety and environmental concerns. They were even able to ensure the nuclear power plant had a pleasing aesthetic that would surely attract the best engineers.

However, as the committee met to deal with the remaining issues, one issue in particular kept popping up: the design of the bike shed for employees that commuted by bicycle.

This included the color, the signage, the materials used, and the type of bike rack to be installed. The committee couldn't get past these details—details that were meaningless in the greater scope of a functioning nuclear power plant. They kept fixating on small, trivial features that were a matter of opinion and subjectivity.

Therein lies the essence of Parkinson's Law of Triviality. People are prone to overthinking and fixating on small details that don't matter in the grand scheme of a task, and they do so to the detriment of larger issues that have infinitely more importance. These are the tasks that, if you were to take a step back and evaluate, would compel you to ask "*Who the heck cares about this?*"

When you lack the clarity and focus to really tackle your big objectives, you start addressing tasks to fit your level of mental energy. You let your tasks run you. It's the classic case of not being able to see the forest for the trees and unwittingly keeping yourself from the finish line. This is especially pronounced when a group is collectively making a decision. Why?

There are two main reasons for this phenomenon.

The first reason is procrastination and avoidance. When people want to procrastinate on an issue, they often try to remain productive by doing something that is perceived as productive. Trivial details are still details that need to be taken care of at some point, and they are things that we can tweak endlessly.

This is why we clean when we are putting off work. We're subconsciously avoiding the work, but making ourselves feel better by thinking, "*At least something productive got done!*"

Fixating on the trivial is the equivalent of cleaning the bathroom to avoid work. You are being productive in some way, but not in a way that aids your overall goal. That's why when the committee members were stuck on how to tackle all of the safety issues, they defaulted to something they *could* theoretically solve: a bike shed.

Trivial tasks need to be addressed at some point, but you need to evaluate when you should actually address them. Triviality can easily sneak into our lives as a placebo for real productivity.

Second, and this refers more to group situations, the Law of Triviality may be the result of individuals who wish to contribute in any way they can, but find themselves unable to in all but the most trivial of matters. They're on the committee, but they don't have the knowledge or expertise to contribute to more significant issues.

Yet everyone can visualize a cheap, simple bicycle shed, so planning one can result in endless discussions, because everyone involved wants to add a touch and show personal contribution. It's completely self-serving.

The main and only reason to call meetings is to solve big problems that require input from multiple people. Locking people in a room and letting them brainstorm is a fairly proven method for getting things done—*if* you have an agenda that you stick to. Anything else should be addressed independently; otherwise the level of discussion inevitably falls to the lowest common denominator in the room.

If somebody starts talking about something that's not on the agenda, you know that triviality is on your doorstep. If somebody is spinning their wheels regarding a tiny aspect of a larger project, triviality is already in the room. If you find yourself suddenly compelled to organize your sock drawer while working on a particularly tough issue, triviality has made a cup of tea and is making itself comfortable.

Be on the lookout for these patterns. When you devolve into small tasks that may not need tweaking, or do not impact your overall goal, it's time to take a break and recharge instead of pretending to be productive.

The key to combatting triviality is threefold: (1) have a strict agenda, whether it is your to-do list or calendar or other technique, so you know what you should focus on and what you should ignore; (2) know your overall goals for the day and constantly ask yourself if what you're doing is contributing to them or avoiding them; and (3) develop an awareness of when you're starting to lose energy so you can pre-empt triviality from occurring.

Knowing is half the battle when it comes to beating Parkinson's Law of Triviality.

Parkinson's other law is simply known as *Parkinson's Law*, and is arguably more well-known. One of the things that people who procrastinate a lot might say to justify it is that they work better under a time crunch—"I work best with a deadline!"

Parkinson's Law states that *work expands so as to fill the time available for its completion*. Whatever deadline you give yourself, big or small, that's how long you'll take to complete work. If you give yourself a relaxed deadline, you avoid being disciplined; if you give yourself a tight deadline, you can draw on your self-discipline.

Parkinson observed that as bureaucracies expanded, their efficiency decreased instead of increased. The more space and time people were given, the more they took—something that he realized was applicable to a wide range of other circumstances. The general form of the law became that increasing the size of something decreases its efficiency.

As it relates to focus and time, Parkinson found that simple tasks would be made increasingly more complex in order to fill the time allotted to their completion. Decreasing the available time for completing a task caused that task to become simpler and easier and completed in a more timely fashion.

Building on Parkinson's Law, a study of college students found that those who imposed strict deadlines on themselves for completing assignments consistently performed better than those who gave themselves an excessive amount of time and those who set no limits at all. Why? The artificial limitations they had set for their work caused them to be far more efficient than their counterparts. They didn't spend a lot of time worrying about the assignments because they didn't give themselves the time to indulge. They got to work, finished the projects, and moved on. They also didn't have time to ruminate on what ultimately didn't matter—a very common type of subtle procrastination. They were able to subconsciously focus on only the elements that mattered in completing the assignment.

Very few people are ever going to require you or even ask you to work less. So if you want to be more productive and efficient, you'll have to avoid falling victim to Parkinson's Law yourself by applying artificial limitations on the time you give yourself to complete tasks. By simply giving yourself time limits and deadlines for your work, you force yourself to focus on the crucial elements of the task. You don't make things more complex or difficult than they need to be just to fill the time.

For example, say that your supervisor gives you a spreadsheet and asks you to make a few charts from it by the end of the week. The task might take an hour, but after looking over the spreadsheet you notice that it's disorganized and difficult to read, so you start editing it. This takes an entire week, but the charts you were supposed to generate would only have taken an hour. If you had been given the deadline of one day, you would have simply focused on the charts and ignored everything that wasn't important. When we are given the space, as Parkinson's Law dictates, we expand our work to fill the time.

Set aggressive deadlines so that you are actually challenging yourself on a consistent basis, and you'll avoid this pitfall. A distant deadline also typically means a sustained level of background stress—push yourself to finish early and free your mind. Save your time by giving yourself less time. Sounds easy, doesn't it?

#25.The Pareto Principle

Back when I was starting my own business, I spent a lot of time spinning my wheels on tasks that didn't matter. This can easily spiral into perfectionism and analysis paralysis, and I was no exception.

Because I wanted everything I produced to impart as much value as possible, I spent an inordinate amount of time on small changes and edits that no one besides me would ever notice. I suppose my head was in the right place, but that's not what makes a business succeed.

The overall message and effectiveness was largely the same, but I would re-work sentences over and over until I was satisfied with them. Consequently, it took almost a year to write and edit my first book.

This isn't to say that quality control isn't important. However, I now realize there's no sense in agonizing over every word choice in a book, especially if the overall message and effectiveness will not change or be improved.

In the vast majority of cases, tinkering with the tiny things won't make a difference. The primary reason is the 80/20 Rule, otherwise known as the Pareto Principle.

The Pareto Principle was named for an Italian economist who accurately noted that 80% of the real estate in Italy was owned by only 20% of the population. He began to wonder if the same kind of distribution applied to other aspects of life. In fact, he was correct.

The Pareto Principle applies to everything about the human experience: our work, relationships, career, grades, hobbies, and interests. Time is your most precious asset, and the Pareto Principle allows you to use it more effectively for maximum rewards. It accurately recognizes that you just might be wasting a significant amount of time on things that make no difference.

The Pareto Principle states that 80% of the results you want out of a task will be produced by 20% of your activities and efforts directed toward it.

In other words, only 20% of the tasks you perform toward a certain goal will account for the vast majority of your results. Conversely, the remaining 80% of the tasks and effort are merely focused on bringing a task to perfection and optimal efficiency. They are mostly unnecessary in the name of high productivity and output, and most of the time they are not worth the effort. Talk about a waste.

In concrete terms, 20% of the tasks you focus on will yield 80% of the results you desire, and any additional tasks you might focus on aren't going to impact your overall productivity that much. Further, 20% of the time you spend on a task will yield 80% of the progress you need, and any additional time spent will create diminishing returns and an overall poor usage of your time.

The tip has a simple proposition: pay attention to only 20% of your tasks, and for those tasks, 20% of the effort you spend on them just might be sufficient for your purposes.

For example, if you set a goal of trying to lose weight, you will lose 80% of the weight by just doing 20% of the actions you think you should, such as eating within certain hours, and hitting the gym three times a week. Everything else, like counting every calorie and lugging around Tupperware filled with broccoli and chicken—that's the 80% effort that will only create 20% of the results. Further, 20% of the time spent on losing weight will yield the bulk of the results, and any more time spent is unnecessary unless you are trying to drop to 4% body fat.

You would just focus on the actions that make the biggest impact and debate whether you want to even touch the others. Seek the biggest bang for your buck. What are the tasks that make the biggest impact, regardless of details or completion? Do those first and foremost—they might be all you need.

Lacking awareness of this phenomenon means you will continue to spin your wheels on 80% of the effort that doesn't impact your bottom line. You will also fail to identify the 20% of your business, tasks, or work that are truly working for you and miss a host of opportunities. This is when time works *against* you.

To maximize your focus, you need to realize there is a point at which working on something won't yield any more results. There's a point beyond which people won't notice the additional work or perfection, and where the purpose of the task is adequately satisfied. For most of us, this point is far earlier and lower than we might expect.

Here's an illustration of how the Pareto Principle impacts real life application.

Language expert Gabriel Wyner says that when you're beginning to learn a new language, focus only on the 1,000 or so most common words in that language first: "After 1,000 words, you'll know 70% of the words in any average text, and 2,000 words provide you with 80% text coverage."

Wyner explains the imbalance even further. Let's say you knew only 10 English words: "the," "(to) be," "of," "and," "a," "to," "in," "he," "have," and "it." If that was the extent of your vocabulary, how much of any text would you recognize?

According to Dr. Paul Nation, the answer is 23.7%. Those 10 words represent 0.00004% of the English language, which has over 250,000 words. But we use those 10 so often that they regularly make up nearly 25% of every sentence we write.

Let's say we eventually increase our vocabulary to a whopping 100 words— including "year," "(to) see," "(to) give," "then," "most," "great," "(to) think," and "there." With that number, Dr. Nation says, we'd have the ability to understand 49% of every sentence uttered.

Let that sink in a bit—with only 100 words, we can recognize nearly half the content of every sentence. Let's be generous and fluff his numbers—that would still mean that with 200 words, we could recognize 40% of the content in each sentence. The fact that *less than one ten-thousandth* of all English words make of almost half of every sentence is kind of a big deal. That is a staggering demonstration of the Pareto Principle.

What tasks do you *really* think people will or won't notice (even if you do)? What additional tasks might others tell you to just skip or disregard? How can you maximize your efficiency by knowing where to cut corners? How can you manage your energy and save your focus for what really matters?

Focus and productivity are never about your best intentions. They are purely results-driven, and the Pareto Principle drives results in the most efficient manner with the time you have.

#26. Maker and Manager Modes

What's a maker and what's a manager? Well, chances are you constantly juggle both roles despite your actual title.

When you're writing a report or analyzing a document, you're a maker. It's when you are producing and creating something— anything. On the other hand, when you're coordinating, planning, or scheduling, you're acting like a manager. You may not have realized it, but these are diametrically opposed roles. To start with, one requires uninterrupted time, while the other one is specifically trying to interrupt schedules.

Consider the daily schedule of novelist Haruki Murakami. When he's working on a novel, he starts his days at 4:00 a.m. and writes for five or six continuous hours. This is his maker mode. Once the writing is done, he spends his afternoons exercising and coordinating with others, and his evenings reading or listening to music before his 9:00 p.m. bedtime. Of course, he spends the rest of his day in manager mode. Why is this so significant?

Paul Graham of technology incubator Y Combinator first described this concept in a 2009 essay. From Graham's distinction between makers and managers, we can learn that doing creative work or overseeing other people does not necessitate certain habits or routines. It requires consideration of the way we structure our time. Namely, it requires us to recognize when we are in either mode, and then split our days accordingly like Murakami.

A manager's day is, as a rule, sliced up into tiny slots, each with a specific purpose decided in advance. Managers spend a lot of time "putting out fires" and doing reactive work. An important call or email comes in, so it gets answered. To focus on one task for a substantial block of time, managers need to make an effort to prevent other people from distracting them.

A maker's schedule is the polar opposite. It is made up of long blocks of time reserved for focusing on particular tasks, or the entire day might be devoted to one activity. Breaking their day up into slots consisting of a few minutes each would be the equivalent of doing nothing. They need to do one thing well and can leave the rest to the managers. Uninterrupted time is truly the currency for a maker.

When you try to mix and match these two modes throughout your day, both modes won't be able to accomplish what they want. Not even close.

For improved focus, alter your schedule to ensure that you are keeping everything maker related together, and everything manager related together. In other words, you should batch the tasks from each mode together so each mode can actually accomplish what they want.

If you have three documents to write and three meetings (interruptions) to hold, how might you structure your day? Suppose you held meetings one hour apart—does that give the maker enough time to get into the zone and create? No. Or, suppose you keep the meetings one right after the other — does that give the manager enough time to react and organize? No.

A better method would be to emulate what Murakami does by devoting your mornings to writing, and then your afternoons to meetings. We all embody these roles from time to time, so set each version of yourself up for success by differentiating and batching maker and manager modes.

#27. Just 10 Minutes

Knowing that our own brain is against us, how can we tap into our inner reserves of focus? Our tendency to procrastinate on large or intimidating projects is reinforced by our imagination. We visualize the worst parts of the task, adding layers of emotion each time we picture ourselves performing it, and that makes it easier to delay getting started. But we can overcome this inertia by implementing the 10-minute rule.

The rule is simple: just commit to starting and sticking with it for 10 minutes. Time is magnificent, endless, and a puzzle—but we can take it 10 minutes at a time and drastically improve our focus.

That's where the 10-Minute Rule comes

in—if you want something, wait at least 10 minutes before getting it. It's simple and leaves no room for debate or excuses. When you feel an urge, force yourself to wait for 10 minutes before giving in to whatever the urge is. If you're still craving it after 10 minutes, then have it, or wait 10 more minutes because you've already done it and survived just fine. Simply by choosing to wait, you remove the "immediate" from immediate gratification, thereby building focus and discipline.

Similarly, if you want to quit something beneficial, wait just 10 more minutes. It's the same thought process applied in a different way. 10 minutes is nothing, so you can wait or continue that long easily. Then, if you do it once, it's easy to repeat, isn't it?

For example, if you'd rather not do the dishes or your homework, that's exactly what you're going to do for at least 10 minutes. You can give yourself permission to quit after 10 measly minutes. Chances are you'll finish the task you were dreading, or eliminate the inertia that was holding you back and not want to stop after 10 minutes. Perfect.

The secret sauce is in immediate action. If you're able to cross this threshold, you'll see that the task itself is not so painful. It was just your sense of laziness and sloth that was holding you back.

You'll surprise yourself with how much more you can get done and how easy it is to build your sense of willpower. The difficult part is creating the snowball, but we all know what happens when you roll it down a hill.

#28. Visualize your Future Self

Remember that the defining feature of procrastination isn't just the act of putting off tasks; it's the deliberate delaying of intended tasks, even while knowing full well that such delay will cause negative consequences in the future. Well, guess who suffers in that scenario? Not being focused isn't just about complacency or mere forgetfulness. It's more about hazarding the welfare of our future selves as we focus on gaining short-term pleasure at the cost of long-term benefits.

Research into chronic procrastination and lack of focus has unearthed an interesting discovery on what sets apart chronic procrastinators from the rest. We each have a way of transporting our mind into the future—we do it whenever we set goals, plan, or bring up positive affirmations. Through these activities, we're able to connect with our future selves and visualize how we're going to transition from our present situation to that future vision.

For chronic procrastinators, though, that vision of their future selves tends to be blurry, more abstract, and impersonal.

They often feel an emotional disconnect between who they are at present and who they'll become in the future.. As they are more strongly in tune with the desires of their present selves and don't feel connected enough with their future selves to care about their welfare, chronic procrastinators also more readily give in to the lure of short-term pleasures. Rather than sacrifice present comfort for future rewards, they choose to revel in what feels good now because their vision tends to be more limited to the immediate moment. Thus, they have a harder time delaying gratification

This is what psychology professor Dr. Fuschia Sirois calls *temporal myopia* (more easily thought of as nearsightedness with regards to time)—a key quality that may largely underlie chronic procrastination.

To further clarify the phenomenon of how our perception of time can influence the way we make decisions, Hal Hershfield, a professor of marketing at UCLA's Anderson School of Management, conducted experiments. Using virtual reality, Hershfield had people interact with their future self. The results of his experiments revealed that people who interacted with their future selves were more likely to be concerned about both their present and future selves, and also tended to act favorably in consideration of their future selves. For instance, they were much more likely to put money in a fake, experiment-based retirement account for the benefit of the future self they interacted with.

What did Hershfield's studies show us? The better we're able to visualize and interact with our future self, the better we get at taking good care of it.

This is because by visualizing and connecting with our future self, we feel the reality of the upcoming circumstances and recognize how the actions of our present self are bound to create a real impact on our future self. For example, if we visualize how failing to prepare well for a seminar we're tasked to organize would impact our future self and its reputation, we're more likely to feel motivated to start planning and acting now.

By practicing visualization, we start to see how procrastinating now may be good for our present self, but disastrous for our future self. As we empathize with the fate of our future self, and the kind of life it will have to live through if we keep up our habit of procrastination (e.g., sleepless nights trying to get caught up with work, turning in haphazardly done output, having to deal with career failures), we begin to feel motivated to change our present ways to be more productive.

So the next time you feel compelled to procrastinate, think of your future self. Travel through time, in a manner of speaking.

Create a vivid image in your mind depicting your future self in a failure scenario and try to feel what they feel in that event. Then picture your future self in a success scenario and try to feel all the positive emotions you'd feel in that moment. Visualize every little step and reaction your future self would make in both situations. Getting a taste of the two alternate lives your future self might experience will increase your motivation to act toward realizing your vision of success, rather than the failure scenario. Make it stick and make it impactful.

As you come to appreciate the beauty of a success scenario, visualize how the completed task looks like, and trace your way back—that is, outline the specific tasks you need to perform to get to that vision of your future self proudly completing the task at hand and reaping its rewards. If you still feel hindered from getting started toward your goal, try to review which of the smaller subtasks is holding you up and why.

As you troubleshoot your lack of motivation to get going, always keep the vision of your future self at the forefront of your mind. It will serve as a reminder both of the positive consequences of beating procrastination, and of the negative impacts of failing to fight the urge to delay your intended tasks.

Takeaways:

- The concept of time is intertwined with focus and productivity. Mostly, we see this relationship as negative because we always seem to be lacking time. But there are a few ways to reset your perspective of time and understand how it can help you, rather than hurt you.

- Protect your time. Your time is precious, and only when you can protect it from others will you realize its true value. You can ward people off who threaten your focus by making them jump through a small hoop to speak in depth with you. If you are ambushed in person, set the tone at preemptively mention that you are busy and have very little time to spare.

- Make the most out of your time by not doing things out of obligation or duty, avoiding negative people no matter their relationship to you, and maximizing your limited leisure time by not being lazy and doing what makes you happiest.

- Parkinson came up with two important laws related to focus and time. First is Parkinson's Law of Triviality, which states that you must see the forest through the trees and not get stuck in small details because they are easy to brainstorm with and kick around. Parkinson's second law is known simply as Parkinson's Law and states that work expands to fill the time it is given. To battle this, proactively set aggressive deadlines and don't allow yourself to be seduced by seemingly free time.

- Manage your maker and manager modes. When you're a maker, you're creating something. When you're a manger, you're coordinating, planning, scheduling, and informing. These are polar opposites in terms of what they require, and thus, you should be aware of the mode you're currently in and batch your mode-specific tasks together.
- Just 10 minutes; that's all it takes sometimes to build focus and jumpstart productivity. If you don't feel like getting started, commit to just 10 minutes. If you feel like quitting, persevere for just 10 minutes. That's all it takes.
- Part of the reason we procrastinate and refuse to focus sometimes is because we are all about our present selves. Our present selves don't want to delay gratification. Of course, our future selves aren't happy with this tendency. Therefore, a surprising way to improve

focus is to visualize your future self in two situations—a positive one where you've done what you needed to do, and a negative one where you've neglected your tasks and are paying the price.

Summary Guide

SECTION 1.TAKE THE FIRST STEP

- Focus is tough, but the toughest part about focus is simply getting started. It's because we all have to deal with a certain amount of inertia to begin our days. Getting into motion from a standstill takes energy, but there are ways to short-circuit the process for yourself.
- First, take note of Newton's law of momentum. This states that when an object is in motion, it tends to stay in motion, and when an object is at rest, it tends to stay at rest. How can you be an object that stays in motion? It starts with how you wake up, begin your day, and don't allow time for inertia to set in.

- Productive mornings go hand in hand with Newton's law. When you can create a galvanizing and energizing morning routine for yourself, you can set the tone you want for the rest of the day. The morning routine that is recommended leaves little to no room for decisions or thought, and depends on planting the seeds of your tasks so you grow anticipation toward them.
- Getting started is easier when you have something small and easy in front of you. After all, it is easier to take a single step versus climb a mountain, even though they both have the same end goal. Therefore, break all of your tasks into smaller sub-tasks, and then do it again. This psychologically makes it easy for you to get started and take action.
- We all know what we should do, roughly speaking. But it's those things that we shouldn't do that sometimes keep us from getting started. We should avoid the sneaky tasks that are secret wastes of time. This should all be encapsulated in a "don't-do" list, where you make sure to note things to ignore and not pay

attention to because they would distract you from what actually matters.

- Finally, motivate yourself into action with rewards. Make sure to use short-term rewards to instantly provide yourself with pleasure after getting started. Pair this with long-term goals that keep you motivated on a deeper level. Both of these have the pleasant side effect of taking the stigma away from your work and creating a positive and happy association with it.

SECTION 2. CREATE AND SEIZE MOMENTUM

- Momentum is a delicate thing. While the first section was focused on getting started, this section is on step two, three, and four, and making sure you capitalize on your hot start. Momentum by itself may be easier to achieve than breaking inertia, but it can slip away in just a moment.
- An easy way for momentum to slip away is through perfectionist tendencies. Perfectionism is nitpicking at every

small detail at the detriment of overall progress. It emphasizes quality over quantity—this by itself isn't negative, but all things in moderation. To boot, the main reason most people engage in perfectionism isn't because of an adherence to excellence—it is because of fear of judgment and rejection.

- Perfectionism will halt you in your steps. So will constantly doubling back and editing, correcting, and tweaking things before you finish 100% of something. Do and complete first, edit later. This doesn't just apply to writing. When you go back to fix or change something, you lose your train of thought and cease to keep going forward. You begin to slide backwards, and by the time you finish editing, you've taken one step forward and two steps back. Completion is almost always your real goal.

- Multitasking is a myth. We've all heard this, but it's time to hear it again. We know that trying to work on several things simultaneously just results in poor quality across the board—most of us avoid this, at this point. However, we still tend to switch between tasks frequently, which is the modern version of multitasking. It takes far longer than you might expect to shrug off a distraction and return to your previous mental state, so defeat multitasking by single-tasking and focusing. If you feel that you need to address something during your single-tasking period, just write it on a distractions list and don't confuse something that's urgent for something that's important.

- Get in the habit of taking notes in general—this simple act frees up your brain for the present moment and doesn't let the future or the past interfere.
- Finally, distraction blackouts can increase your momentum because they force you into a state of boredom and isolation. When you're bored, you have a choice to remain bored, or begrudgingly work on what's in front of you. Intentionally put yourself into an uncomfortable situation, and you'll come out the other side in a better position. Use competition against yourself as an

additional motivator. Make sure to schedule a distraction blackout during your time of greatest daily energy and efficiency.

SECTION 3. HOW TO STAY FOCUSED

- We may be past the difficult first part, as well as the delicate second part, but that doesn't mean we're out of the woods yet. How can we remain focused on a long-term basis? What can we intentionally enact and effectuate, versus just identifying pitfalls to avoid?
- First of all, you should be aware of and take advantage of your circadian rhythm. Studies have shown that during both sleep and waking periods, our bodies run in 90-minute cycles. This means that no matter what, your focus will wane after about 90 minutes. Use this knowledge strategically and be sure to not burn out by pushing too hard. Listen to your body and manage your energy instead of your time.

- Chewing gum has oddly enough been proven to help focus. Staying fueled and hydrated should be less surprising. The brain represents 20% of our body's energy consumption, so it needs to be constantly replenished and hydrated.

- An implementation intention is just an *if-then* statement. For example: *If* it is 10:00 a.m., *then* you will ignore emails for two hours. It takes away your choice and free will. This is actually good, because our present selves often lack the foresight to make optimal decisions.

- Nature is a powerful, curious thing. Natural light, simply seeing green, watching baby animals, and having plants around have all been shown to increase focus and productivity.

- Sometimes what you need to get focused in a change of environment and context. This simply refers to moving locations when your focus and energy are dipping. It helps because there is a certain amount of alertness that a new environment brings because of the new stimuli. Memory has also been shown to improve when learning while being exposed to different settings.

- Finally, doodling has been shown to help focus. This is because doodling essentially acts as an outlet for your frustration, boredom, and desire to procrastinate. Yet it does so in a way that is low-impact and allows you to keep focusing and thinking on a matter at hand.

SECTION 4. PLAN STRATEGICALLY AND OUTSMART YOURSELF

- Sometimes we just don't have the willpower to focus as we like. This may often be the case, actually. Thankfully, we have the opportunity to plan against our worst tendencies and guarantee that we are doing what we need to do in a timely manner.
- The first way to plan strategically for focus is by diagnosing your focus. This is paying attention to how well you can pay attention. At some point, you will just need to take a loss for the day and

stop completely. This break prevents burnout, and is actually much more preferable to grinding it out and trying to forge ahead at 50% mental capacity. You just won't get much done, you'll create a negative association with hard work, and you'll waste your time. Know when to cut your losses!

- A daily goals checklist you can think of as a to-do list. Create this the night before so you can think clearly and objectively, instead of emotionally and in reaction to your day. This list decreases your stress because you've got everything laid out and nothing will fall through the cracks. For each day, create a mixture of easy and difficult tasks so you can program in mental breaks. Finally, be a little bit aspirational in your daily workload.

- Instead of a to-do list, you can categorize your tasks. This is helpful because it provides greater context to what you should be focusing on. There are five categories: Immediate Attention, In Progress, Follow-up, Upcoming, and Ideas. Don't move to the next category until you finish everything in the current one.

- Similarly, you can organize your tasks by using ABCDE priorities. The priority levels are determined on the consequences you will receive. "A" and "B" levels have negative consequences and "C" is a bonus, while "D" and "E" have positive benefits.

- For a more three-dimensional and thorough look at your tasks, try scheduling them all in your calendar. This takes significant work beforehand, but it takes your life, habits, tendencies, and energy levels into account. You do not live in a vacuum, and your calendar can reflect this.

- Finally, you can arrange your environment to assist your ability to focus by manipulating your default decisions. Default decisions are what humans will do most of the time just because they are easiest and cost us the least effort. You can make your distractions cost you more effort, and make focus as easy as sitting down.

SECTION 5. MAKING TIME YOUR FRIEND

- The concept of time is intertwined with focus and productivity. Mostly, we see this relationship as negative because we always seem to be lacking time. But there are a few ways to reset your perspective of time and understand how it can help you, rather than hurt you.

- Protect your time. Your time is precious, and only when you can protect it from others will you realize its true value. You can ward people off who threaten your focus by making them jump through a small hoop to speak in depth with you. If you are ambushed in person, set the tone at preemptively mention that you are busy and have very little time to spare.

- Make the most out of your time by not doing things out of obligation or duty, avoiding negative people no matter their relationship to you, and maximizing your limited leisure time by not being lazy and doing what makes you happiest.

- Parkinson came up with two important laws related to focus and time. First is Parkinson's Law of Triviality, which states that you must see the forest through the trees and not get stuck in small details because they are easy to brainstorm with and kick around. Parkinson's second law is known simply as Parkinson's Law and states that work expands to fill the time it is given. To battle this, proactively set aggressive deadlines and don't allow yourself to be seduced by seemingly free time.
- Manage your maker and manager modes. When you're a maker, you're creating something. When you're a manger, you're coordinating, planning, scheduling, and informing. These are polar opposites in terms of what they require, and thus, you should be aware of the mode you're currently in and batch your mode-specific tasks together.
- Just 10 minutes; that's all it takes sometimes to build focus and jumpstart productivity. If you don't feel like getting started, commit to just 10 minutes. If

you feel like quitting, persevere for just 10 minutes. That's all it takes.

- Part of the reason we procrastinate and refuse to focus sometimes is because we are all about our present selves. Our present selves don't want to delay gratification. Of course, our future selves aren't happy with this tendency. Therefore, a surprising way to improve focus is to visualize your future self in two situations—a positive one where you've done what you needed to do, and a negative one where you've neglected your tasks and are paying the price.

·

CPSIA information can be obtained
at www.ICGtesting.com
Printed in the USA
FSHW020702140221
78616FS